悦读丛书

浙江省社科联人文社科出版全额资助项目

浙江省社科规划一般课题
——18KPCB03YB——

U0749155

大型国际会议双语指南

——浙江对话世界

杨佩佩 著

浙江工商大学出版社
ZHEJIANG GONGSHANG UNIVERSITY PRESS

图书在版编目(CIP)数据

大型国际会议双语指南:浙江对话世界 / 杨佩佩著
. — 杭州:浙江工商大学出版社,2018.6
ISBN 978-7-5178-2717-7

Ⅰ. ①大… Ⅱ. ①杨… Ⅲ. ①国际会议–指南 Ⅳ.
①D813–62

中国版本图书馆 CIP 数据核字(2018)第 082006 号

大型国际会议双语指南——浙江对话世界

**Bilingual Guide to Large International Conferences:
Zhejiang's Dialogue with the World**

杨佩佩 著

责任编辑	刘淑娟　任晓燕
封面设计	林朦朦
责任印制	包建辉
出版发行	浙江工商大学出版社
	(杭州市教工路 198 号　邮政编码 310012)
	(E-mail:zjgsupress@163.com)
	(网址:http://www.zjgsupress.com)
	电话:0571–88904980,88831806(传真)
排　　版	杭州朝曦图文设计有限公司
印　　刷	杭州五象印务有限公司
开　　本	710mm×1000mm　1/16
印　　张	11.25
字　　数	195 千
版 印 次	2018 年 6 月第 1 版　2018 年 6 月第 1 次印刷
书　　号	ISBN 978-7-5178-2717-7
定　　价	35.00 元

Preface Ⅰ | 序一

Nowadays, as a vital platform for China's voice on international stage, Large International Conferences (hereinafter LICs), play a critical role in disseminating China's voice and nurturing its discourse power. In recent years, Zhejiang has become a popular host of many international conferences, which creates opportunities for the international development of the province and its cities as well as the cultural exchanges with foreign countries. At this point in time, *Bilingual Guide to Large International Conferences: Zhejiang's Dialogue with the World*, has been listed as the research finding of one key popularization project by Zhejiang Provincial Association of Social Science. This book, from the perspective of the LICs held in Zhejiang Province, presents a bilingual, readable, practical, and public-oriented guide in order to meet internationalization requirements of individual readers and urban development.

大型国际会议,作为目前中国在国际舞台上发声的重要平台,对传播中国声音、抢占话语权力来说,扮演着至关重要的角色。近年来,浙江省举办了许多国际会议,这为浙江省的国际化发展、文化的对外交流造就了乘势而上的契机。恰逢其时,《大型国际会议双语指南——浙江对话世界》一书,被列为浙江省社科联社科普及重点课题的研究成果。本书以浙江省举办的大型国际会议为切入视角,以满足读者个人和城市发展的国际化需求为目标,是一部双语对照、耐读实用、面向大众的科普读物。

Above is why I have confirmed the significance of publishing this book. As to the author's invitation to me on writing a preface, I accepted with alacrity, mainly due to the following two reasons. Firstly, since I have been engaged in the study of cultural discourse and international communication, I am quite pleased to see such a professional and practical guide from Ms. Yang Peipei. Secondly, as a Zhejiang local, same with the author, I am proud of the fact that our province and cities are able to host more and more LICs. Besides, I also hope to contribute to our province and cities' march to the world stage.

这是我对本书出版意义方面的肯定。而作者邀我为该书作序,我欣然同意,主要有以下两个原因。首先,本人从事的是文化话语和国际传播交流研究,看到杨佩佩老师的这本专业实用指南当然十分高兴。其次,作为一名浙江人,我和作者一样,为我们的浙江省能够成功举办越来越多的大型国际会议而感到自豪,也希望为促进浙江省走向世界舞台贡献一份力量。

During the communication with the author, I could feel that her knowledge and perception are closely related to the process of writing this book. I also heard that she had worked on temporary post for one year in the Foreign Affairs Office of Hangzhou Municipal Government, and participated in the preparatory work for the G20 Hangzhou Summit during the whole processes, in which she had received a lot of training for etiquette and conference affairs. Therefore, this book is based on real materials and authentic experiences with certain credibility.

在与作者的交流中,我感受到她的学识和感悟与本书的创作息息相关。作者在杭州市人民政府外事办公室挂职一年,全程参与了G20峰会的筹备工作,期间也接受了许多涉外礼仪和会务方面的培训。因此,本书取材真实,具备一定的公信力。

If you have never read about or participated in a LIC and just want to uncover its mysterious veil; or if you already have relevant or similar experiences and want to further develop the different aspects and features of LICs, you can open this book, follow the words step by step and take time for your own contemplation. Here I would like to share some reflection on the book from the following three aspects.

如果读者从未了解或参与过大型国际会议,只想近距离揭开它的神秘面纱;抑或有相关或类似的经历,并想进一步了解它的不同方面和特征,都可以打开书卷,听作者娓娓道来,细细品味。这里我想从以下三个方面来谈谈我对本书的认识。

Firstly, the book is relatively well organized. Three chapters are respectively displayed from the basic chapter of LICs to the key content of conference preparation, volunteer service and foreign etiquette, then to the service of food and accommodations, venue performances and other tours. Therefore, the layout is reasonable with different levels properly stated and the key point clearly presented. In addition, the organization of subsections in each chapter is also rich and well arranged.

第一，全书的编排较有条理。三大章节从大型国际会议的基础篇，到会议筹备、志愿服务、涉外礼仪等重要内容篇，再到食宿和会场演出、观览等服务篇，编排合理、层次得当、重点突出。此外，每个章节内部各个小节的设置也是丰富多彩又井然有序。

Secondly, the content is complete, accurate, and understandable. Many parts of the book, especially the semi-structured interviews towards staff, the dialogue cases of conference preparation and volunteer service and foreign etiquette, etc., are materials based on real situations. Each subsection begins with a brief introduction, moves on with bilingual key words and sentences extracted from the introduction, and combines with situational practices, interviews or extensive links according to different section focuses, all of which are developed from simple to difficult with both theory and practice.

第二，内容翔实，深入浅出。书中许多内容，特别是对工作人员的半结构式访谈、会议筹备和志愿服务的对话案例、涉外礼仪等，均为立足于真实场景的素材。每一小节由简介开始，然后摘录简介中重要词汇和句子的双语对照，根据各小节不同侧重辅以情景演练、访谈或拓展链接等板块，由简入难，将理论知识与实战演练相结合。

Thirdly, this book keeps pace with the times and fits a wide range of people. In recent years, in terms of Zhejiang Province, no matter the G20 Hangzhou Summit, or the annual World Internet Conference in Wuzhen, or even the coming Asian Games which has already started its preparatory work, they all ask the related staff, service people, students and citizens to acquire relevant knowledge to different degree. In addition to Zhejiang, some like Beijing and Shanghai are also favored by LICs. Therefore, as for individual readers, this book can be used not only as bilingual training materials or a reference manual, but also as an empirical book for a large number of readers to enhance their ability of international communication. For Zhejiang

Province, it can provide some references for the preparation of the future LICs.

第三，与时俱进，受众较广。近年来，仅从浙江省来说，无论是 G20 峰会，还是一年一度的乌镇世界互联网大会，抑或已经启动筹备工作的亚运会，都需要相关工作人员、服务行业、大学生和广大市民不同程度地去学习相关知识。除了浙江以外，北京、上海等也备受大型国际会议青睐。如此一来，对个人来说，本书既可作为双语培训教材或参考手册，又可作为广大读者提升国际交流能力的实效读物。对浙江省来说，可为其筹备未来的大型国际会议提供一定的借鉴。

President Xi Jinping has been stressing, "Tell China's stories and spread China's voice well." It calls for joint efforts of every reader. We sincerely hope this book will be helpful to you.

习近平总书记强调："讲好中国故事，传播好中国声音。""讲好中国故事，传播好中国声音"需要各位读者的共同努力。希望本书能对广大读者朋友有所帮助。

This is the preface.

是为序。

Changjiang Distinguished Professor　Shi Xu

"长江学者"特聘教授 施　旭

March 28，2017

2017 年 3 月 28 日

Preface II | 序二

The Dialogue at the Right Time
恰逢其时的对话

When the manuscript of the book came to me, four words immediately jumped into my mind—"at the right time." Although the G20 Hangzhou Summit came to a successful ending in September, 2016, its sparkling glow still shines on this ancient but modern city—Hangzhou. Hangzhou is one of the best examples to show that a high-level international conference can promote the overall strength of a city and raise its reputation over the world. When we review the processes of G20 Hangzhou Summit, an unprecedented international event in Hangzhou, we shall think about how many treasures remained are worthy of writing down on the paper and how many spillover effects can be seized for sustainable development. The "Post-G20 Era" put forward by the Hangzhou Municipal Government is just the best footnote to this, and a new city position is clearly displayed in front of us.

当这本书稿来到我面前的时候,我的脑海里立刻跳出了"恰逢其时"这四个字! 虽然 G20 杭州峰会已在 2016 年 9 月圆满落下帷幕,但它发出的熠熠光芒仍照耀在杭州这座古老而现代的城市之上。一场高级别的国际会议提升了一座城市的综合实力,提高了一座城市的世界知名度,杭州就是一个最好的例子。当我们回顾 G20 杭州峰会这场史无前例的国际盛会之际,想一想有多少沉淀下来的珍宝值得我们书写? 有多少溢出效应值得我们抓住供可持续发展? 杭州市政府提出的"后 G20 时代"便是对此最好的注脚,一个全新的城市定位清晰地展现在我们面前。

As early as in the 1950s, smart Hangzhou locals found a similar temperament between Hangzhou and the world famous city—Geneva. Then it has become a long-cherished wish for several generations of Hangzhou locals to make Hangzhou the "Oriental Geneva." Over the past few decades, if we only compare the landscapes of the two cities, the gap has already been very small. However, in terms of other indicators such as the international reputation, the number of Hangzhou-headquartered international organizations and Hangzhou-hosted international conferences, and their matched hardware facilities, service support, etc., there is still a long way for Hangzhou to catch up with Geneva. The success of G20 Hangzhou Summit has truly reflected the subtleties of "challenges and opportunities."

早在 20 世纪 50 年代,敏锐的杭州人就找到了杭州与世界名城日内瓦之间某种相似的城市气质。把杭州打造成"东方日内瓦"是几代杭州人的夙愿。几十年过去了,如果光从湖光山色来比较两座城市,杭州与日内瓦之间的差距已经很小。但从国际知名度、国际组织总部的设立数量、举办国际会议的场次,以及与之配套的硬件设施、服务保障等指标来衡量的话,杭州与日内瓦仍差距甚大。G20 杭州峰会的举办,真实地反映出"挑战与机遇"的微妙之处。

In fact, Hangzhou had not yet undertaken a real conference with international influence before the G20 Hangzhou Summit. The hosting of G20 Summit is undoubtedly a great leap forward for Hangzhou. Fortunately, we have the Zhejiang spirit and Hangzhou spirit, just as the old saying goes, "The wave riders stand on the tides, the red flag in hands won't get wet." Since ancient times, Qian Tang (one of Hangzhou's names in history) has had many "wave riders" generation by generation. So in front of such a key challenge of securing and serving the G20 Summit, Zhejiang locals not only completed the task excellently, but also saved countless valuable conference experience as well as explored and created a new China-style way for hosting LICs. The publication of *Bilingual Guide to Large International Conferences*: *Zhejiang's Dialogue with the World* is one of the classic examples.

事实上,G20 杭州峰会之前,杭州市还没有承接过真正意义上具有国际影响力的会议。G20 峰会在杭州举办对杭州而言无疑是一次巨大的飞越。好在我们有浙江精神、杭州精神,正如人们常说的那样,"弄潮儿向涛头立,手把红旗旗不湿"。钱塘自古"弄潮儿"辈出,在保障与服务 G20 峰会如此重大的挑战面前,浙江人不仅出色地完成了任务,还积攒了无数宝贵的办会经验,探索和创造出一条具有中国特色的举办大型国际会议的新路子。《大型国际会议双语指南——浙江对话世界》一书的出版便是其中一个典型的例子。

This book is originated directly from the hard moment when Hangzhou started its G20 summit projects at the very beginning. It is said that everything is difficult at the beginning. At that time, the difficulties mainly lay in the lack of experience. Even if there was some experience, it was acquired only by a few professionals, most of whom were confined to their own respective fields of work. There wasn't any systematic and complete manual or theoretical book at that moment. Ms. Yang Peipei, a young teacher at School of Foreign Languages, Zhejiang Gongshang University, was one of the earliest key staff transferred to the G20 Hangzhou Summit Accreditation Center. Although Ms. Yang has been teaching English for only a few years, her English skills are quite solid-grounded. Meanwhile, she has an innate passion for work, which can infect her team. The more valuable point is that, in the initial stages of the preparation for the G20 Summit, Ms. Yang has already realized that there was still some vacancy in Hangzhou's experiences of hosting LICs. Through much harsh exploration, she found out that within the whole China, even in the internationalized first-tier cities such as Beijing, Shanghai, and Guangzhou, there was no work manual both systematic and operable, not to mention a public reader.

这本书的诞生直接缘起于 G20 杭州峰会最初启动项目的那段艰难时刻。都说万事开头难,难就难在缺乏经验,即使有,也只被少数从业人员掌握,大多也是仅局限于他们各自的工作领域,没有形成系统、完整的工作手册或理论读本。浙江工商大学外国语学院青年教师杨佩佩是最早一批被抽调至 G20 杭州峰会注册中心的骨干之一。杨老师虽然从教只有几年,但已具备非常扎实的英语功底。她对工作有着与生俱来的热忱,并能以此感染她的团队。更可贵的是,杨老师在 G20 峰会筹备工作的最初阶段就意识到,杭州在举办大型国际会议的工作中尚存在空白。经过一番艰难的跋涉,她发现即便在全国范围内,包括像北京、上海、广州那样的国际化一线城市也没有一本既有系统性,又有可操作性的工作手册,更不用说普及型的读本了。

Oriented from this problem, Ms. Yang Peipei had been diligent and dedicated to her work at the G20 Hangzhou Summit Accreditation Center. As an English teacher, she had limited contact with LICs before her temporary post. Everything had to start from scratch, and time was also limited. She seized all opportunities to learn by listening to lectures, asking other experts, attending series of meetings in other cities, studying materials and organizing her team in real exercises. So within the shortest time, Ms. Yang grew from a green hand to an expert. Team buddies would like to call her "Chief Commander."

杨佩佩老师以问题为导向。在 G20 峰会注册中心工作期间,她是一个既用功又用心的人。作为英语教师的她,在被抽调之前,对大型国际会议的接触是非常有限的。一切都得从头开始,而时不我待。她抓住一切可以学习的机会,通过听讲座,求教于专家,赴其他城市观摩会议,钻研材料,带领团队实景演练。就这样在最短的时间里,杨老师从一名门外汉变成了专家,团队的小伙伴们喜欢叫她"总攻"。

She held the ambition of planning to write a book to promote the work. Then she collected, regularized, settled and refined all available information from the massive first-hand materials she could have access to, just like a miner carefully prepared the tool and waited for the moment of "gold digging." On the one hand, this book did not simply pile up ready-made materials or rewrite them. On the contrary, many materials are drawn from the author's real personal involvement in the project. For instance, many situational practices and semi-structured interviews in the book come from the real frontline scenes during the G20 Hangzhou Summit. Such vivid, first-hand examples can be found in many passages of this book. We can say that the author completed a deep "field investigation" during her post for the G20 Hangzhou Summit and rose abruptly based on the accumulated strengths.

她以计划写本书的雄心来推进手中的工作,从平时接触到的海量办会信息中,收集、规整、梳理、提炼一切可用的资料,如同矿工精心准备着工具,等待挖掘"金矿"的那一刻。一方面,本书的素材不是对现成的材料进行简单堆砌和改写。相反,许多素材均出自作者亲身参与的项目,如书中包含的许多场情景演练和半结构式访谈都来自 G20 峰会期间真实的一线工作场景。如此鲜活的第一手的资料在本书中可谓俯拾皆是。可以说,作者在服务于 G20 峰会期间,厚积薄发,完成了一次深度的"田野考察"。

Another merit of this book is the Sino-English bilingual way of writing.

Taking her language advantages, the author created an "international style" for this book. The English narration does not only improve the level of this book, but also broaden its practicability as to foreign-related issues. As we know, the knowledge involved in a LIC is encyclopedic, which includes politics, diplomacy, economy, finance, energy, education, health care, environmental protection, city traffic and other global hot topics.

采用中英文双语写作是本书的又一大亮点。作者凭借语言优势,把本书的"国际范"做得非常彻底。英文写作的加入,不仅提升了本书的档次,更拓宽了它的涉外实用性。要知道,大型国际会议所涉及的知识点包罗万象,包含了当今世界的政治、外交、经济、金融、能源利用、文化教育、医疗卫生、绿色环保、城市交通等全球性热点话题。

A LIC has a unique set of international code. There are standard routines and professional terminologies for no matter the agenda of the conference or the signs in a venue. As to these, not everyone knowing English well can express it accurately. For example, the coordinator in the G20 Summit is called "Sherpa," while the three carriages (the former host country, the current host country and the next host country) are called "Troika." Those who have not experienced it will never find their exact translation. While in this book, the author makes her best effort to sort out a long list of professional words, phrases and sentences at the end of each chapter, in order to provide readers with convenient learning practice. We can imagine the troubles and challenges the author met during the G20 Summit, which have been transformed into the essence of the book after her concrete experiences, and unreservedly shared with the readers who may also encounter the same problems.

大型国际会议有专属的一套国际规则,大到会议议程,小到会场内的一块指示牌都有标准套路和专业术语。不是每一个熟练掌握英语的人都能准确无误地表达出来。比如,G20峰会中的协调人被叫作"Sherpa",而三驾马车(前任举办国、当前举办国和下任举办国)被叫作"Troika"。没有亲历过这些的人,永远也找不到它们精准的翻译。而在本书中,作者在每一章的结尾处都不遗余力地整理出一长串专业词汇、短语和例句,为读者提供了实实在在的学习便利。可以想象,作者在参与G20峰会服务工作中遇到的麻烦与挑战,经过真枪实弹地实践都已经转化成本书的精髓,并毫无保留地分享给可能也会遇到同样问题的读者。

As a reader for LICs, in the beginning we might be worried that there was certain limitation by only referring to Zhejiang. However, after going through the book, we feel that it is unnecessary for this kind of concern. This book starts from a general introduction of LICs, then analyzes the status quo about the holding of LICs worldwide, and integrates the situation of Zhejiang within it to make the readers understand the position of Zhejiang is in this field without nagging comments. From point to area, the author skillfully built up the bridge from Zhejiang to the outside world. What's more, the addition of Hangzhou elements, including the comments from several foreign visitors and the local customs of Hangzhou, has enhanced the interest of this book.

读者或许认为,作为一本介绍大型国际会议的读本,仅围绕浙江做文章似有某些局限之处。但通读全书后,我们感到这种担忧是多余的。作者从介绍国际会议知识入手,分析了当今全球范围内国际会议举办的现状,又将浙江的现状融入其中,不加点评便让读者知晓浙江在该领域中处于世界的什么位置了。作者以点带面,巧妙地打通了浙江与世界的桥梁。加入的杭州元素,包括几位外国游客对杭州的评价以及杭州的风土人情等,更增强了本书的趣味性。

In a word, *Bilingual Guide to Large International Conferences*:*Zhejiang's Dialogue with the World* is not only a training book for professionals, volunteers of international conferences, college students and English fans, but also a public reading book for spreading knowledge on international conferences. When we are in Zhejiang during a "Post-G20 Era" and a "Pre-Asian-Games Era," the book comes into existence "at the right time." Since a large number of international conferences are approaching, we would rather say that the world is eagerly looking forward to communicating with Zhejiang or China, rather than that Zhejiang is having a dialogue with the world.

总而言之,《大型国际会议双语指南——浙江对话世界》是一本既可作为从业人员、国际会议志愿者、大学生、英语爱好者的培训教材,也可作为传播国际会议知识的普及型读本。当我们身处"后 G20 时代"和"前亚运会时代"之际的浙江,本书的出现"恰逢其时"。一大波大型国际会议正朝我们涌来,与其说是浙江与世界的对话,不如说是世界正迫切地期待与浙江的对话、与中国的对话。

Here comes the preface.

是为序。

Executive Deputy Director of G20 Hangzhou Summit
Accreditation Centre
Zhang Li
G20 杭州峰会注册中心常务副主任 张　励
April 4，2017
2017 年 4 月 4 日

Foreword | 前　言

As the host country for more and more Large International Conferences, China has been increasingly expanding its influences over global management, and grabbing the right to formulate international rules. As the domestic host province for many LICs, Zhejiang has been gradually developing its conference and exhibition industry as well as tourism, and improving the comprehensive level of the province and the overall quality of the public. Zhejiang, apparently through the LICs, has opened a gorgeous dialogue with the world, and will continue to write chapters that are more splendid. Even so, to "enhance the level of city internationalization," it not only proposes challenges to the conference staff's level of internationalization, but also some requirements to the intellectual accomplishment of volunteers and citizens.

作为越来越多大型国际会议的主办国,中国日益拓展了全球治理发言权,抢抓了国际规则制定权;作为诸多大型国际会议的国内主办省,浙江日益发展了会展、旅游业,提高了本省综合水平和市民综合素质。浙江,已然通过举办大型国际会议,开启了和世界的华丽对话,并将继续谱写更美丽的篇章。即便如此,要"提升城市的国际化水平",不仅对会议工作人员的国际化水平提出了挑战,也要求广大志愿者、市民具备一定的知识素养。

As a temporary post member of Hangzhou Municipal Government, I participated in the preparations for the G20 Summit. Through material collection in the real practice, I am more deeply aware of the necessity to spread the theoretical and practical knowledge of LICs. How to help the staff to effectively acquire practical English expressions and foreign-related etiquette for LICs in order to improve the ability to host conferences, and how to help volunteers and citizens to get common knowledge of the Summit in order to enhance citizens' international image, are the missions of this book.

　　笔者作为挂职市政机关单位的一员，参与了 G20 峰会的筹备工作，通过实践中的资料收集，更为深刻地意识到普及大型国际会议及其实务知识的必要性。如何帮助工作人员有效掌握实用的大型国际会议英语表达和涉外礼仪知识，提高办会能力，如何帮助广大志愿者、市民了解峰会常识，提升市民国际化形象，是本书的宗旨所在。

　　Therefore, the main target readers of this book are the conference staff, service personnel and volunteers for LICs, and other citizens and college students interested in this field. This book can be used not only as bilingual training materials or a reference manual for staff and volunteers of LICs, but also as an empirical book for other readers to help to enhance their ability of international communication. At the same time, with the processing of the preparatory work of the Asian Games in Hangzhou, this book can provide some reference for the preparation of the Asian Games and other high-level international conferences in Zhejiang.

　　因此，本书主要读者为大型国际会议的筹备工作人员、服务接待人员、志愿者及其他感兴趣的市民和大学生。本书既可作为高端国际会议工作人员和志愿者的双语培训教材或参考手册，又可作为帮助其他读者提高国际交流能力的实效读物。同时，随着杭州亚运会筹备工作的启动，本书也可为亚运会及浙江省其他高端国际会议的会务筹备提供一定的借鉴。

　　As mentioned above, the book is inspired not only by work practices, but also by the current vacancy of bilingual manual for LICs in the market. The basic writing structure is taking the LICs hosted by Zhejiang and their conference affairs as the center and the bilingual narration as the writing form, with vivid situational practices and real interviews, thus trying to be relatively understandable. Among them, the extract of the key words, phrases and sentences intends to help readers find useful English expressions. In the writing processes, this book mainly adopts two methods: situational practice construction and semi-structured interview. The construction of practical situations or dialogues consistent with the context of each chapter enables readers to have self-exercises while reading, thus combining theoretical knowledge with real practices; the semi-structured interviews to staff and volunteers on their work experiences and reflections enable readers to share with frontline practitioners, thus cultivating a certain international vision.

如上所述,本书的创作灵感不仅来自工作实践,也来自目前市面上针对大型国际会议的双语读本的空缺。创作的基本思路是以浙江省举办的大型国际会议和承担的会务工作为中心,采用双语表达的编写形式,辅以生动的实践情景和真实访谈,深入浅出。其中重点词汇、短语和例句的摘选,将帮助读者找到实用的英语表达方式。在创作过程中,本书主要采用了情景演练构建和半结构式访谈两种方法。构建结合章节内容的实践情景或对话,使读者在阅读的同时还可以进行自我演练,让理论知识落地并增强实用性;对工作人员及志愿者就工作经历和感受进行半结构式访谈,能使读者分享到一线工作的心得体会,培养一定的国际视野。

The book is divided into three chapters:"Approaching Large International Conferences in Zhejiang Province" "Building a Capital of International Conferences in Zhejiang Province" and "Hangzhou Welcomes You: Bilingual Information of Tours." These three chapters are arranged progressively as the chapters of common sense, main body and service, along with appendixes and a reference in the end.

全书分为"走近浙江的大型国际会议""打造省内的国际会议之都"和"浙江欢迎您:资讯出行双语通"三个章节,按常识篇、实物篇和服务篇的顺序依次递进,结尾有附录和参考文献。

The first chapter popularizes basic knowledge of LICs in a Sino-English way, analyzes the market conditions and lists the LICs which has been or will be held in Zhejiang. Then taking the G20 Hangzhou Summit as an example, it introduces venues and the structure of the organization committee. Key words, phrases and sentences for each topic are extracted and relevant situational dialogues are designed with extensive links in the end.

第一章用中英文普及大型国际会议基本知识,分析市场行情,罗列目前和未来几年在浙江省内举办的大型国际会议,并以 G20 峰会为例介绍会场和筹备组织架构;针对每个主题罗列重点词汇、短语和例句,创设主题情景对话,提供拓展链接。

The second chapter is the main body of this book with rich content. It introduces in details the status quo and prospects of building Hangzhou as a capital for international conferences in the Post-G20 Era, as well as the preparatory work, the volunteer service, the internationalization of hotels and the foreign-related etiquette of a LIC. In addition to the regular parts same with the ones of Chapter 1, Subsection 2.1 sets up a new column of the foreign guests' messages, while 2.2, 2.3 and 2.4 set up semi-structured interviews towards staff and volunteers respectively.

第二章为本书重点,内容丰富,详细介绍了后 G20 时代杭州关于打造国际会议之都的现状和前景,以及大型国际会议筹备工作、志愿服务、酒店的国际化建设和涉外礼仪。除了保留第一章中的常设栏目之外,本章 2.1 小节新设了外宾留言一栏,2.2,2.3 和 2.4 小节新设了对工作人员及志愿者的半结构式访谈一栏。

The third chapter mainly focuses on the usability by providing a variety of information and a travel guide of Hangzhou. It begins with a general overview of basic necessities, goes on with the viewing guide to the Hangzhou International Expo Center (HIEC) and the "Impression on West Lake" show, and then with the culinary recommendation from the G20 Hangzhou Summit as well as public services and medical information, etc.

第三章专注于实用性,主要提供各种资讯和出行指南,先以杭州衣食住行概况总起,然后具体展开杭州国际博览中心和印象西湖的观影指南,之后推介了峰会宴席菜品,提供了杭城公共服务和医疗信息等。

The appendixes mainly include the keynote speech of important leaders and their translations, and a selection of G20 Leaders' Communique Hangzhou Summit.

附录部分内容主要包括重要领导致辞及其讲稿译文和 G20 杭州峰会公报选读。

This book is the research finding of one key popularization project by Zhejiang Provincial Association of Social Science in 2016 named "A Practical English Guide for Large International Conferences". Here I would like to express my acknowledgement to my colleagues and friends who has been caring about or helping the writing of this book. Special thanks go to Prof. Shi Xu and Director Zhang Li for the prefaces, Ms. Yang Xianju and Ms. Chen Chan for consultation and the two postgraduate students Ms. Wang Lingwei and Mr. Zhang Zaihao for their assistance. Hopefully it will provide the conference staff, service personal, volunteers and other citizens and college students interested in this field with a book combining the functions of a guide, a manual as well as a literature for reference. In view of the author's limited level, if there is any omission or inappropriateness in this book, please forgive and point out for the author!

本书为 2016 年浙江省社科联社科普及重点课题"大型国际会议实用英语指南"的研究成果。特此感谢关心和帮助过本书编写的同事和朋友们！特别感谢施旭教授和张励主任为此题序,感谢杨仙菊老师和陈婵老师提供咨询,感谢研究生王玲炜、张载浩的帮助。谨此希望为大型国际会议的筹备工作人员、服务接待人员、志愿者及其他感兴趣的市民和大学生提供一本兼具手册、读物和参考文献功能的书籍。鉴于水平有限,若有疏漏和不妥之处,敬请谅解与指正!

Yang Peipei

杨佩佩

May 30，2017

2017 年 5 月 30 日

CONTENTS | 目录

Chapter 3　Hangzhou Welcomes You: Bilingual Information of Tours 杭州 欢迎您：资讯出行双语通

Appendixes 附录

References 参考文献

Chapter 1

Approaching Large International Conferences in Zhejiang Province

走近浙江的大型国际会议

1.1 What are Large International Conferences
什么是大型国际会议

1.1.1 Brief Introduction 简介

According to the standards by International Congress and Convention Association (ICCA), conferences held in more than 3 rotatory countries with more than 50 attendants are defined as International Conferences. Relatively speaking, this is an official and accurate definition of International Conferences. Then what is the definition of a Large International Conference? Due to the variety of cognition and values of different places and organizations all over the world, it's hard to specifically define a LIC. However, based on the definition of International Conference, the scale of a LIC should be clearly defined as larger than 3 rotatory countries and 50 attendants. It mainly refers to a multilateral assembly aiming to solve international issues of much concern and coordinate mutual benefits, thus searching or adopting joint actions (such as passing resolution, reaching agreements and signing treaties) based on common discussion.

根据国际大会及会议协会(ICCA)统计国际会议的标准,至少在 3 个国家轮流举行且与会人数至少 50 人的固定性会议属于国际会议。以上为国际会议较为官方和准确的定义。那么什么样的国际会议才可以称为大型国际会议?由于世界各地和各组织的认知和价值观不同,目前很难明确地界定。但基于国际会议的定义,我们可以明确大型国际会议的规模必定在轮值国为 3 个、参会人数为

50 人之上,主要是指多国代表为解决共同关心的国际问题、协调彼此利益,在共同商议的基础上寻求或采取共同行动(如通过决议、达成协议、签订条约等)而举行的多边集会。

The preparation work of a LIC generally includes initiation of the conference, choices of its time and location, invitation for participants, drawing-up of the agenda, documents sorting and other related technical issues (such as seating arrangement and names of delegations from different countries, etc.). Careful preparation lays a good foundation for the success of the conference.

大型国际会议的筹备一般包括会议的发起、会议召开的时间和地点的选择、会议的邀请,以及会议议程的拟定、会议文件的整理和有关的技术性问题(如与会各国代表团的座次安排、名称的使用等)。周密的准备工作可为会议的成功奠定良好的基础。

LICs are usually held in a city of the sponsoring country, or alternately in a city of the participating countries, or in some neutral locations like Geneva, Switzerland and Vienna, Austria, etc. In many cases, for the host country, hosting international conferences means that its international status has been affirmed by the rest of the world, or even its international influence has been expanded. Since the beginning of the 21st century, with the professionalization, marketization and internationalization of China's conference industry, more and more LICs have been held in China. China's capacity of conference-organizing has been increasingly recognized around the world.

大型国际会议的地点通常选在发起国的某一城市,或轮流在各参加国的某一城市举行,抑或在一些中立地点(如瑞士的日内瓦、奥地利的维也纳等)举行。多数情况下,举办国际会议对东道国来说意味着世界其他国家对其国际地位的肯定,甚至可以扩大其国际影响。21 世纪以来,随着我国会议产业的专业化、市场化、国际化水平的不断提高,越来越多的国际性大会来中国举办,我国的会议组织能力也越来越得到全世界认可。

The invitation of LICs is generally issued by the host country, or sometimes by the non-host sponsor country. A draft of procedural rules and a description of participating requests in the Conference should be attached to

Figure 1-1   Word Internet Conference(Wuzhen Summit)

图 1-1   世界互联网大会(乌镇峰会)

the invitation letter. The organization forms of international conferences vary with their size and issues. Some conferences only have a plenary meeting (namely a general assembly), yet many other conferences include plenary meetings and panel meetings (namely committees) or even occasionally with special committees. An international conference always produces some specific outcomes which will be announced in the form of documents including resolutions, agreements, declarations, treaties, contracts or final documents. Treaties and contracts of the Conference need to be signed by the representatives of participating countries, and ratified by a certain required number of delegations before coming into force.

大型国际会议的邀请一般由会议主办国发出,有时由非主办国的发起国发出。在发出邀请信之时,应附有一份拟议中的程序规则草案,并说明参加会议的要求。因其举行规模及讨论问题的不同,往往有不同的组织形式。有些会议只有全体会议(即大会),但大多数会议分为全体会议和小组会议(即各委员会),有时还设立特别委员会。国际会议结束后总有一定的结果,其具体形式往往表现为会议的文件,如决议、协议、宣言、条约、和约或最后文件。会议的条约、合约一般须经各国代表签字,并得到法定数量的国家的批准后才能生效。

1.1.2 Words, Phrases and Sentences 词汇、短语和例句

Large International Conference (LIC) 大型国际会议

International Conference and Convention Association (ICCA)国际大会及会议协会

be held in turns/rotation 轮流举行

reaching agreements and signing treaties 达成协议、签订条约

initiation of the conference 会议的发起

drawing-up of the agenda 会议议程的拟定

documents sorting 会议文件的整理

professionalization, marketization and internationalization 专业化、市场化、国际化

host country 主办国

a plenary meeting (namely a general assembly) 全体会议(即大会)

panel meeting (namely committee) 小组会议(即各委员会)

(1)According to the standards by International Congress and Convention Association (ICCA), conferences held in more than 3 rotatory countries with more than 50 attendants are defined as International Conference.

根据国际大会及会议协会(ICCA)统计国际会议的标准,至少在3个国家轮流举行且与会人数至少50人的固定性会议属于国际会议。

(2)Then what is the definition of a Large International Conference?

那么什么样的国际会议才可以称之为大型国际会议?

(3)Careful preparation lays a good foundation for the success of the conference.

周密的准备工作可为会议的成功奠定良好的基础。

(4)Treaties and contracts of the Conference need to be signed by the representatives of participating countries, and ratified by a certain required number of delegations before coming into force.

会议的条约、合约一般须经各国代表签字,并得到法定数量的国家的批准后才能生效。

1.1.3 Situation Practice 情景演练

A：Hi! What are you doing? You look so concentrated!

B：I'm searching for some materials on Large International Conferences. As you know, our department is assigned to help our municipal government to host the International Friendship Cities Forum next year. Since it's my first time to deal with stuff in this field and I've no idea about Large International

Conferences, I need to learn about it.

A: What a coincidence! Last year I took part in an international academic conference. At that time, I also read some related books and learned a lot from the real practice of conference preparation.

B: That's awesome! Would you mind sharing with me how a Large International Conference is normally conducted? What should I do to prepare for it?

A: The preparation for a Large International Conference is really a long course! It not only involves the initiative, time, location and invitation of the conference, but also the drafting of conference programs, the sorting of conference documents and relative technological problems. You'll see once you are assigned with a specific task.

B: Our department should be responsible for the invitation of the conference.

A: Nowadays international conferences are always using e-mails to send invitation letters. So I think during e-mail communication, the procedures, rules and requirements of the meetings should be made clear in the letter or as an attachment.

B: Thanks so much! I can feel what you've mentioned will help me a lot. Next time could you please recommend some materials for me?

A: My pleasure! Of course, I'll look for some and give you next time.

A：在干什么呢？这么认真！

B：我在找一些关于大型国际会议的资料。我们单位要配合市政府办好明年的国际友好城市论坛。我是第一次接触这方面的工作,对大型国际会议完全没有概念,需要了解一下。

A：这么巧！我去年参与过一个国际学术会议的工作。当时我也读了一些这方面的书,并且在会议筹备的实践当中学到了很多。

B：那太好了！你和我说说看,大型国际会议到底是个什么概念。我现在该做哪些功课呢？

A：大型国际会议的筹备可是一门大学问！它包括会议的发起、会议召开时间和地点的选择、会议的邀请,以及会议议程的拟定、会议文件的整理和有关的技术性问题。到时候看你具体负责哪一块。

B：我们应该是负责会议邀请。

A：现在国际会议一般都是通过电子邮件发邀请函的。我觉得在发邀请函的时候，应该把会议的程序规则和参会要求也简单写一下，或者加在附件里。

B：非常感谢！我觉得你说的都对我有很大的帮助，下次能不能推荐一些资料给我看看？

A：不客气！可以啊，下次我找一些给你看。

1.2 How Many Large International Conferences Held in Zhejiang Do You Know
浙江大型国际会议知多少

1.2.1 Brief Introduction 简介

According to the Statistics from ICCA, China held 333 international conferences in 2015 and kept ranking 2nd in Asian-Pacific region from 2014. As shown in Figure 1-2, the top 10 cities of Mainland China in the World's Best Conference City rank were Beijing, Shanghai, Hangzhou, Guangzhou, Nanjing, Chengdu, Xi'an, Shenzhen, Wuhan and Xiamen. Here the one particularly emphasized is Hangzhou—capital of Zhejiang Province. Hangzhou held 27 international conferences in 2015, and ranked 3rd in Mainland China, 24th in Asia and 100th in the world. It is the first time that Hangzhou has ascended to the top 100 international conference destinations in the world. However, while counting the conferences already held in Zhejiang Province and the upcoming ones, how much do you know about them?

国际大会及会议协会(ICCA)统计显示，中国于 2015 年共举办 333 场国际会议，维持了自 2014 年以来亚太地区第二的排名。如图 1-2 所示，中国大陆入围全球最佳国际会议城市的前十名依次为北京、上海、杭州、广州、南京、成都、西安、深圳、武汉和厦门。特别值得一提的是，浙江的省会城市——杭州于 2015 年凭借 27 个国际会议，位列全国第 3 位，亚洲第 24 位，全球第 100 位。这也是杭州首次跻身全球 100 强国际会议目的地城市行列。那么对于那些年在浙江举办过和即将举办的大型国际会议，你又知道多少呢？

(1)2016 G20 Hangzhou Summit 2016 年 G20 杭州峰会

The Group of Twenty (G20) was established in the G7 Finance Ministers'

中国十强（内地）

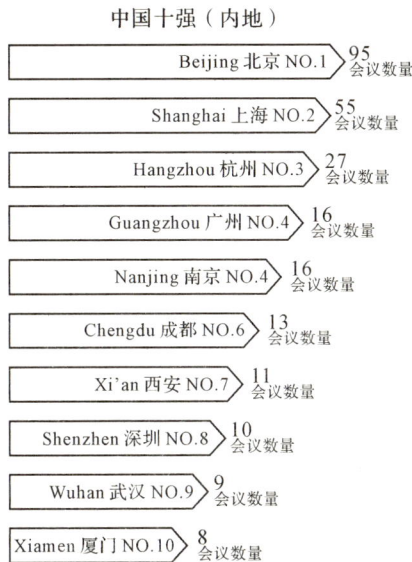

Figure 1-2 Top 10 cities of Mainland China in the World's Best Conference City rank

图 1-2 中国大陆入围全球最佳国际会议城市的前十个城市

Conference in 1999. The members include 20 Groups—Argentina, Australia, Brazil, Canada, China, France, Germany, India, Indonesia, Italy, Japan, South Korea, Mexico, Russia, Saudi Arabia, South Africa, Turkey, United Kingdom, United States and the European Union (EU). Before the outbreak of the international financial crisis in 2008, there was only the G20 Finance Ministers and Central Bank Governors Meeting in which delegates exchanged views on international financial and monetary policies, the reform of international financial systems and world economic development. America advocated developing G20 as a leader summit after the financial crisis. Today the G20 mechanism has formed a structure with the summit as the leading, "Two-track Mechanism" — Sherpa channel and Financial channel as the support, the Ministerial Meeting and the Working Group as the auxiliary.

二十国集团(G20)由七国集团财长会议于1999年倡议成立,由阿根廷、澳大利亚、巴西、加拿大、中国、法国、德国、印度、印度尼西亚、意大利、日本、韩国、墨西哥、俄罗斯、沙特阿拉伯、南非、土耳其、英国、美国和欧盟共20方组成。2008年国际金融危机爆发前,G20仅举行财长和央行行长会议,就国际金融货币政策、国际金融体系改革、世界经济发展等问题交换看法;2008年国际金融危机爆发后,在美国倡议下,G20提升为领导人峰会。目前,G20机制已形成以峰会为引领、协调人和财金渠道"双轨机制"为支撑、部长级会议和工作组为辅助的框架。

Up to now, the G20 Summit has already been held 11 times and the 11th summit was held in Hangzhou, China from September 4 to 5, 2016.

G20迄今已举行了11次峰会,第11次峰会于2016年9月4日至5日在中国杭州举行。

(2)World Internet Conference (Wuzhen Summit) 世界互联网大会(乌镇峰会)

World Internet Conference (WIC) is held in the city of Wuzhen, Zhejiang Province annually by the Cyberspace Administration of China and Zhejiang Provincial Government, which had its first conference from November 19 to 21, 2014, when it attracted prominent Internet figures from nearly 100 countries. This was China's first Internet conference of this kind and on this scale, which is unparalleled even globally.

一年一度的世界互联网大会由中国国家互联网信息办公室和浙江省人民政府在乌镇联合主办。2014年11月19日至21日的第一届大会就吸引了来自近100个国家的互联网巨头。这是中国举办第一场如此大规模的互联网大会,甚至在全世界来讲都是无与伦比的。

The Internet is causing a revolution that will reform and influence human development and it creates economic growth and more convenient lifestyles. But it also poses unprecedented challenges, such as unequal development, cyber insecurity, uneven distribution of key resources, and new risks from new technology.

互联网正在发起一场影响和改变人类发展的革命,同时带来了经济增长和更方便的生活方式。但它也带来了史无前例的挑战,比如发展不平等、网络不安全、核心资源分配不平衡及新兴技术带来的新的风险。

(3)2022 Asian Games in Hangzhou 2022年杭州亚运会

The 19th Asian Games will be held in Hangzhou, China, from September 10 to 25, 2022. Hangzhou is the 3rd Chinese city to host the Asian Games. The 11th Asian Games was held in Beijing in 1990 while the 16th Asian Games was held in Guangzhou in 2010. Hangzhou Asian Games will set up 41 events, including 33 Olympic projects and 8 non-Olympic projects. Hangzhou will also hold the 4th Asian Para Games after the Asian Games.

第 19 届亚洲运动会将于 2022 年 9 月 10 日至 2022 年 9 月 25 日在中国杭州举行,杭州是中国第三个取得亚运会主办权的城市。北京曾于 1990 年举办第 11 届亚运会,广州曾于 2010 年举办第 16 届亚运会。杭州亚运会设 41 项比赛项目,包括 33 个奥运项目和 8 个非奥项目。杭州还将在亚运会后举办第四届亚洲残疾人运动会。

1.2.2 Words, Phrases and Sentences 词汇、短语和例句

top 100 international conference destinations 全球 100 强国际会议目的地
international financial crisis 国际金融危机
Finance Ministers and Central Bank Governors Meeting 财长和央行行长会议
monetary policy 货币政策
Two-track Mechanism 双轨机制
working group 工作组
World Internet Conference (WIC)世界互联网大会
unparalleled even globally 在全球来讲无与伦比的

(1) It is the first time that Hangzhou has ascended to the top 100 international conference destinations in the world.

这也是杭州首次跻身全球 100 强国际会议目的地城市行列。

(2) Today the G20 mechanism has formed a structure with the summit as the leading, "Two-track Mechanism"—Sherpa channel and Financial channel as the support, the Ministerial Meeting and the Working Group as the auxiliary.

目前,G20 机制已形成以峰会为引领、协调人和财金渠道"双轨机制"为支撑、部长级会议和工作组为辅助的框架。

(3) But it also poses unprecedented challenges, such as unequal development, cyber insecurity, uneven distribution of key resources, and new risks from new technology.

但它也带来了史无前例的挑战,比如发展不平等、网络不安全、核心资源分配不平衡及新兴技术带来的新的风险。

1.2.3 Extensive Links 拓展链接

G20 峰会官网 https://www. g20. org/Webs/G20/DE/Home/home _
node. html

世界互联网大会官网 http://www. wicwuzhen. cn

中国奥委会官网 http://www. olympic. cn

1.3 Ways to Approach Venues and Organization Structure
会场和组织架构的正确打开方式

1.3.1 Brief Introduction 简介

1.3.1.1 Venues 会场

After focusing on these international conferences, we shall have a look at
what kind of venue in Hangzhou is honored to be the primary venue for LICs.
That is the Hangzhou Olympic & International Expo Centre. It mainly consists
of the Hangzhou International Expo Centre (HIEC) and the main stadium.

在一饱这些国际会议的眼福之后,让我们来看看在杭州是什么样的场馆才
能有幸作为大型国际会议的主场馆。那就是杭州奥体国际博览中心。杭州奥体
国际博览中心主要由杭州国际博览中心和主体育场两部分构成。

Figure 1-3　Hangzhou International Expo Centre (HIEC)
图 1-3　杭州国际博览中心

First and foremost, HIEC needs to be introduced. It has been put into use
since 2016 as the primary meeting venue for G20 Hangzhou Summit. The HIEC

is located at No. 353 Benjing Avenue, Qianjiang Century City, Xiaoshan District, Hangzhou. It is about a 15 minutes' drive from the Hangzhou Xiaoshan International Airport. Covering 190 thousand square meters of land, it features in total five exhibition sub-centers, equipped with a conference center, a rooftop garden, commercial amenities, an underground retailing mall and parking area. The conference center has a total of 50 meeting venues that range in size from 50 to 3300 square meters. Guided by the building concept of Majestic Grandeur, the HIEC assimilates into its design the elements of a sloping roof, silk decoration, lanterns and wood carvings that are characteristic of Southern China's architectural style. Embodying environmental friendliness, its stately exterior is in harmony with the refined, composed indoor space, conveying both the masculine awe of northern land and the poetic beauty of Southern China.

首先隆重登场的是杭州国际博览中心(简称国博中心)。2016 年国博中心投入使用并成为 G20 杭州峰会的主场馆。国博中心位于杭州市萧山区钱江新城奔竞大道 353 号,距离萧山国际机场 15 分钟车程。它占地 19 万平方米,由五个展览中心组成,设有会议中心、屋顶花园、商务场所、地下零售和停车场。会议中心共有 50 个大小不一的会议场地,从 50 平方米到 3300 平方米不等。在雄伟壮丽的建筑理念指导下,国博中心将倾斜的屋顶、丝绸、灯笼和木雕这些设计元素融合一体,体现了中国南方的建筑风格。国博中心注重环保,其富丽堂皇的外表与精致的室内空间和谐交融,既传达了中国北方的魁梧气概,又展示了南方的诗意之美。

During the G20 Hangzhou Summit, the HIEC is the venue for:

(1) Leaders' plenary session

(2) Official welcome

(3) Official photograph

(4) Leaders' working lunch on Monday, 5th September

(5) Press conference by President Xi Jinping

在 G20 杭州峰会期间,杭州国际博览中心是以下活动的会场:

(1)领导人全体会议

(2)官方欢迎仪式

(3)官方合影

(4)9 月 5 日周一领导人工作午宴

(5)习近平总书记的新闻发布会

The following facilities and services are available at the HIEC：

(1)Leaders' plenary room

(2)Leaders' lounge

(3)Simultaneous interpretation for all leaders' plenary session and working lunch

(4)Delegation office

(5)Bilateral meeting room (available on a booking system via e-mail or Liaison)

(6)Delegate viewing/listening room

(7)Delegate dining

(8)Media center

(9)Press conference room

(10)Media dining

(11)Prayer room

(12)Medical room

(13)Wireless Internet

杭州国际博览中心有以下会议设备和服务可供使用：

(1) 领导人全体会议室

(2) 领导人休息室

(3) 领导人全体会议和工作午宴的同声传译

(4) 代表团办公室

(5) 双边会议室(通过邮件或联络官预约)

(6) 代表听会室

(7) 代表晚宴

(8) 媒体中心

(9) 新闻发布会议室

(10) 媒体晚宴

(11) 祈祷室

(12) 医疗室

(13) 无线网络

Secondly, let's learn something about the main stadium. It was put into use before the National Students' Sports Meeting in 2017. Its appearance looks like a "lotus bowl" and the huge adoption of green low-carbon technology embodies the concept of "Green Olympic Expo." In the large underground space of the main stadium, by the application of fallen-square design with light pipe technology, the mode of natural lighting is fully adopted, thus reducing artificial lighting. As a result, the underground space features an energy-saving, low-carbon and naturally-lit environment. According to the small distance between the Olympic Expo Centre and the Qiantang River, the geographical conditions are fully utilized to adjust the temperature of the main stadium and sports swimming pool by heat pump technology using river water, thus achieving energy conservation and low carbon. In addition, the Olympic Expo Centre is also designed with the real-time measurement and monitoring of energy consumption as well as its display system. As for the lighting, air-conditioning, elevators, water supply and drainage energy, the real-time measurement and monitoring of energy consumption for each building can improve the level of energy reduction with effective operation management. "The use of these technologies is expected to bring the Olympic Expo Centre in Hangzhou a 10.3% reduction in energy consumption and a 15.4% reduction in carbon dioxide emission compared with normal green parks."

然后,我们一起来认识一下主体育场。它在 2017 年全国学生运动会召开前交付使用。它的外形犹如一只"莲花碗",大量绿色低碳技术的采用体现了"绿色奥博"的理念。主体育场的大面积地下空间,通过下沉式广场设计光导管技术应用,充分采取自然采光方式、尽量减少人工照明,构建节能低碳、光环境舒适的地下空间。根据奥体博览城紧邻钱塘江的地理位置,因地制宜,充分运用江水源热泵技术来调节主体育场和体育游泳馆的温度,达到节能低碳的目的。此外,整个奥体博览城还设计了建筑运行能耗实时计量监测与展示系统,根据照明、空调、电梯、给排水等能耗用途,实时计量监测各栋建筑的能源消耗情况,从而提高节能运营管理水平。"这些技术的运用,预计可使杭州奥体博览城绿色园区,相对常规园区建筑能耗水平降低 10.3%、二氧化碳排放量减少 15.4%。"

Figure 1-4   Main Stadium

图 1-4 主体育场

1. 3. 1. 2 Organization structure 组织架构

In contrast to the formal mechanisms set up through legal methods by international organizations, G20 adopts an informal mechanism which relies on member countries' consensus in the pursuit of common goals. There are no standing secretariats or staff. The presidency is under a rotation system and a temporary secretariat is set up by the rotating presidency to coordinate the group work and organization of the event. China is the rotating presidency of the 11th Summit. The Finance Ministers and Central Bank Governors Meeting is held once a year while Ministerial-level Meetings and the Leaders' Summit are usually held at the end of the year. In addition, the Working Group Meetings are needed to discuss the adjustment for the time of those conferences based on actual need.

不同于由国际组织通过法律制定的方式建立起来的正式机构,G20 采用非正式机构,依靠成员彼此所追求目标之间能够达成的共识来组建,没有常务秘书处和工作人员。主席采取轮换制,由轮值主席国设立临时秘书处来协调集团工作和组织会议。中国是第 11 届峰会的轮值主席国。财长和央行行长会议每年一次,部长级例会和首脑峰会通常在年末举行,根据实际需要调整时间,成立工作组,召开工作会议。

G20 has adopted an "open & flexible" mechanical structure: Leaders' Summit—Sherpa Meeting—Ministerial-level Meeting—Expert Working Group Meeting. A temporary secretariat is set up by the rotating presidency, following the negotiation principle of reaching consensus and keeping a good interactive relationship with non-member countries. The term "Troika" usually heard about in LICs also plays an important role in the G20 mechanism. In LICs, the term "Troika" refers to the rotating presidency last year, this year and next year. As to the G20 Summit in 2016, Turkey, China and Germany have formed the "Troika" as the 12th G20 Summit was held in Germany in 2017.

G20采用"开放、灵活"的机制架构:峰会—协调人会议—部长级会议—专家工作组会议。由轮值主席国设立临时秘书处,遵循协商一致的议事规则,并与非成员保持良好互动的关系。我们平时听到大型国际会议中常提到的"三驾马车",在 G20 机制里面也起到了重要作用。在大型国际会议中所谓的"三驾马车",是指去年轮值国、今年轮值国和明年轮值国。对于 2016 年 G20 峰会来说,即土耳其、中国和德国。第 12 届峰会于 2017 年在德国举办。

Under the slogan "A Good Host, A Better G20," all the government departments of Zhejiang Province cooperated to build an organizational structure named as "One Office with Nine Departments" and the Art Show Committee. The "One Office" refers to the summit's preparatory office mainly composed of provincial and municipal key leaders; under the leadership of the "One Office", nine departments carry out the work as planned and targeted. They respectively are Venue Department 1, Environmental Protection & Venue Department 2, Hotel & West Lake Security, Urban Improvement & Traffic Security, News & Media Department, Culture & Activities Department, Health Care & Volunteer Services, International Economic Cooperation Department and Security Department. In addition, the Art Show Committee is in charge of "Impression on West Lake" show.

在"办好 G20,当好东道主"的口号下,浙江省各个政府部门通力合作,构建起"一办九部"+艺术指导委员会的组织架构。"一办"是指峰会筹备办公室,主要由浙江省重要领导构成;在"一办"的领导下,九个部门有规划有目标地开展工作。九个部门分别为:场馆保障一部、环保行动与场馆保障二部、宾馆与西湖景区保障部、城市环境提升与交通保障部、新闻宣传部、文艺活动部、医疗卫生与志愿者服务部、国际经济合作部和安全保卫部。此外,艺术指导委员会主要负责峰会晚会之"印象杭州"的演出。

On the other hand, as to the Asian Games in the near future, on March 18, 2016, "General Office of the State Council's Agreement on the Set-up of the

19th Asian Games Organizing Committee in 2022 by the State Council's Office" agreed to set up the 19th Asian Games Organizing Committee (hereinafter referred to as the committee) and its composition. Chair of the committee was assigned to Mr. Liu Peng, chief of National Sports Bureau, and Mr. Li Qiang, provincial governor of the people's government of Zhejiang Province. On April 9, 2016, the founding meeting of the 19th Asian Games Organizing Committee was held in the Zhejiang Great Hall, Mr. Xia Baolong, secretary of provincial party committee and director of the provincial standing committee, and Mr. Liu Peng, chief of National Sports Bureau, jointly inaugurated the 19th Asian Games Organizing Committee.

另一方面,对于即将到来的亚运会,2016 年 3 月 18 日,《国务院办公厅关于同意成立 2022 年第 19 届亚运会组委会的函》同意成立 2022 年第 19 届亚运会组委会(以下简称组委会)及其组成。组委会主席由体育总局局长刘鹏、浙江省省长李强担任。2016 年 4 月 9 日,2022 年第 19 届亚运会组委会成立大会在浙江省人民大会堂举行,浙江省委书记、省人大常委会主任夏宝龙与国家体育总局局长刘鹏共同为第 19 届亚运会组委会揭牌。

Figure 1-5　Stadium of the 19th Asian Games
图 1-5　第 19 届亚运会场馆

1.3.2 Words, Phrases and Sentences 词汇、短语和例句

primary venue 主会场
Hangzhou International Expo Centre (HIEC) 杭州国际博览中心
a temporary secretariat 临时秘书处
the rotating presidency 轮值主席席位

leaders' lounge 领导人休息室

simultaneous interpretation 同声传译

bilateral meeting room 双边会议室

delegate viewing/listening room 代表听会室

press conference room 媒体发布会议室

Finance Ministers and Central Bank Governors Meeting 财长和央行行长会议

Sherpa Meeting 协调人会议

Troika "三驾马车"

One Office with Nine Departments "一办九部"

jointly inaugurate 共同揭牌

National Sports Bureau 体育总局

the 19th Asian Games Organizing Committee 第 19 届亚运会组委会

(1) After focusing on these international conferences, we shall have a look at what kind of venue in Hangzhou is honored to be the primary venue for LICs.

在一饱这些国际会议的眼福之后,让我们来看看在杭州是什么样的场馆才能有幸作为大型国际会议的主场馆。

(2) Embodying environmental friendliness, its stately exterior is in harmony with the refined, composed indoor space, conveying both the masculine awe of northern land and the poetic beauty of Southern China.

国博中心注重环保,其富丽堂皇的外表与精致的室内空间和谐交融,既传达了中国北方的魁梧气概,又展示了南方的诗意之美。

(3) The use of these technologies is expected to bring the Olympic Expo Centre in Hangzhou a 10.3% reduction in energy consumption and a 15.4% reduction in carbon dioxide emission compared with normal green parks.

这些技术的运用,预计可使杭州奥体博览城绿色园区,相对常规园区建筑能耗水平降低 10.3%、二氧化碳排放量减少 15.4%。

(4) On April 9, 2016, the founding meeting of the 19th Asian Games Organizing Committee was held in the Zhejiang Great Hall, Mr. Xia Baolong, the secretary of provincial party committee and director of the provincial standing committee, and Mr. Liu Peng, chief of National Sports Bureau, jointly inaugurated the 19th Asian Games Organizing Committee.

2016 年 4 月 9 日,2022 年第 19 届亚运会组委会成立大会在浙江省人民大会堂举行,浙江省委书记、省人大常委会主任夏宝龙与国家体育总局局长刘鹏共同为第 19 届亚运会组委会揭牌。

Chapter 2

Building a Capital of International Conferences in Zhejiang Province

打造浙江省内国际会议之都

2.1 Hangzhou's Vitality in Post-G20 Era
后 G20 时代杭州"动"起来

2.1.1 Brief Introduction 简介

Millions of meetings are held in different parts of the world every year. But only the host cities of those meetings often catch the world's attention. The world-renowned "meeting capitals" includes Geneva, Paris, Brussels and New York, etc. Taking Geneva as an example, it is Switzerland's third largest city, but it is more famous than the capital city, and even known as "capital of the planet."

全球每年有数以万计的会议在不同地方召开,人们的目光往往聚焦到这些会议举办地。全球知名的"会议之都"包括瑞士日内瓦、法国巴黎、比利时布鲁塞尔、美国纽约等。以日内瓦为例,日内瓦是瑞士的第三大城市,然而它比瑞士首都更加有名,甚至有"地球的首都"之称。

There are many reasons for being an international conference capital. For example, Geneva is a typical tourist city, located in the center of Europe with convenient transportation. However, the influence of politics and culture contribute more to Geneva's international status. Switzerland became a permanent neutral state in the Vienna Conference in 1815, which not only protected Switzerland from the the First World War and the Second World War, but also made Geneva a center for all nations to solve the world's problems. Now when it comes to Hangzhou, how can it be vitalized through the opportunity of LICs?

　　能够成为国际会议之都,原因有很多。比如,日内瓦是典型的旅游城市,位于欧洲中心,交通方便。然而能够成为国际会议之都,更多的还是因为它的政治与文化。1815 年,维也纳会议确立了瑞士永久中立国的地位,这不仅使瑞士在两次世界大战中免受战乱,还让日内瓦成了为全人类解决问题的中心。那么杭州如何借大型国际会议之契机"动"起来呢?

　　With the success of the G20 Summit in 2016, the popularity and influence of Hangzhou have been "vitalized" rapidly. Compared to Geneva and other renowned international "meeting capitals," Hangzhou has both disadvantages and its own unique advantages. "Hangzhou is the world's most beautiful, luxury city." Italian traveler Marco Polo's description may also represent a lot of westerners' first impression of Hangzhou. Hangzhou, same as St. Petersburg, the G20 Summit host city in 2013, has a long history. Hangzhou is also a charming tourist attraction like the G20 Summit host in 2015, Antalya, Turkey. At the same time, Hangzhou also has a wealth of experience in hosting large-scale international conferences, such as the successful holding of the Fifth International ARGO Science Group meeting and 2015 Global Women Entrepreneurs Conference, and so on. But in terms of popularity, there is a big gap between Hangzhou and Beijing, Shanghai and other first-tier cities in China. G20's influence is enormous as each year's global economic contentious issues and future economic trends are discussed in this meeting. G20 Summit will greatly enhance the influence and international status of Hangzhou. Therefore, Hangzhou needed to seize the opportunity of hosting the G20 Summit to promote itself to the world.

　　随着 2016 年 G20 峰会的成功举办,杭州的知名度与影响力都迅速"动"起来了。相对于日内瓦等国际知名"会议之都",杭州存在不足也有自己得天独厚的优势。"杭州是世界上最美丽华贵之天城。"意大利旅行家马可波罗的描述或许也是很多西方人对于杭州的第一印象。与 2013 年的 G20 峰会举办地——俄罗斯城市圣彼得堡一样,杭州拥有悠久的历史。和 2015 年的 G20 峰会举办地——土耳其城市安塔利亚相似,杭州也是一座魅力无穷的旅游城市。与此同时,杭州也拥有丰富的大型国际会议举办经验,比如成功举办了第五次国际 ARGO 科学组会议、2015 全球女性创业者大会等。但就知名度而言,杭州与北京、上海等一线城市相比还有较大差距。G20 的影响力是巨大的,每一年的全球经济热点、未来经济走向都将在这个会议上加以商讨。G20 峰会将大大提升杭州的城市地位和国际影响力。也正因为如此,杭州更需要抓住此次举办 G20 的契机,向全世界推介自己。

For example, in order to realize the slogan "A Good Host, A Better G20," city construction and its infrastructure had also been "vitalized." Among them, public bicycles of Hangzhou had a largest overhaul ever to match with the Summit (completed by the end of 2016). After upgrading of the public bicycle system, the functions of self-assist search machines had been improved greatly, thus making the operation more convenient.

比如,为落实"办好 G20,当好东道主"的口号,杭城建设和公共设施也"动"起来了。其中,为助力 G20 峰会,杭州公共自行车迎来了史上的最强升级(于 2016 年底前完成)。升级后,服务点内自助查询机的功能有很大提升,操作起来也更加方便自如。

The major upgrading of the bicycle system lies in the humanistic concern. The new function of "returning bikes overnight" makes bicycles' renting and returning more convenient. Clicking "inquiry about surrounding stops" can help to search bicycle availability of the surrounding 5 stops, thus facilitating users to rent and return bicycles nearby.

本次主要的系统升级体现在人性化关怀上。"隔夜还车"新功能让租还车变得更方便。如点击"附近站点查询",可以查询周边 5 个站点的车辆空满情况,方便就近租还车。

Figure 2-1　Public Bicycles in HangZhou

图 2-1　杭州公共自行车

In the past, while you were renting a bike, if you didn't have enough balance remained, you couldn't return the bike. You had to put more money into your card first, and then call the artificial hotline to have your card reset. That's too inconvenient. After upgrading, you can charge your card by paying online. In the meantime, the system had been improved to allow a faster return process once the user tends to return the bicycle.

以往,若租车时遇到余额不够,还不了车的麻烦事,只能先充值,再致电公共自行车热线,由人工进行卡片重置,非常麻烦。升级后,只要通过网上支付方式,就能充值成功。同时,系统的改进大大加快了用户的还车流程。

It is reported that there are more than 3,500 service stops in the main urban areas. 250 of them have finished the upgrading before February, 2016, and 90 of them are located in the Binjiang district.

据悉,主城区共有3500多个服务点,截至2016年2月已完成250个服务点的升级,其中90个服务点在滨江区。

Another example, in the preparation of the G20 Summit, Hangzhou, for the first time, started the systematic upgrading work of the whole city lighting. It's not only lighting for three core scenic areas of West Lake, the Grand Canal and Qiantang River, but also the "dressing up" for the primary roads and 10 city entrances. With the overall lighting show on, Hangzhou looked like a beautiful "city that never sleeps" integrating "the ink and wash landscape into the southeast China."

再比如,为了准备G20峰会,杭州首次启动全城系统化亮化提升工作,不仅围绕西湖、运河、钱塘江三大核心景区进行景观灯光提升工作,还将对重要道路及10个入城口进行亮化"装扮"。当整个亮化工程展示之时,杭州仿佛融合了"水墨江南"的美丽"不夜城"。

During the preparation, the West Lake lighting mainly focused on the south route and three islands in the lake. The lights along West Lake and three islands were connected as a spectacle and controlled by light sensors. It looked pleasant and mysterious by varying from different angles and scenes at any time.

G20准备期间的西湖亮化提升工作,主要针对南线和湖中三岛。西湖沿线的灯光和湖中三岛的灯光连成一片,以光感智能控制,各种角度、各种场景随时整体变换,非常奇妙。

As to the Qiantang River lighting project, it was reported that the Qiangjiang new CBD and the Olympic Expo Center were taken as the core with the extension to the west area of Hangzhou. Usually the lighting was static, while during the festival, the light linkage could be fully utilized by the node buildings to demonstrate Hangzhou's culture through dynamic lighting of varying scenes.

关于钱塘江亮化提升工作,据报道,它主要以钱江新城和奥体中心为核心向西延伸,平日以建筑静态灯光为主,节庆期间可通过节点建筑实现灯光联动,通过动态灯光画面演绎杭州文化。

Besides, the lighting upgrading of the canal focused on improving the overall lighting from Wulin Gate to Qingfang Bridge. It aimed to create the visual effect which enables it vary from the scenery of fishing boat lights decorating bridges in the rain to the sparkling river along ten miles, and to "small bridges with houses by the river." Therefore, the canal had become a night route with both refined and popular tastes.

另外,本次运河亮化提升主要针对运河的武林门至轻纺桥段进行整体灯光改造提升。它旨在营造诸如渔火点点的江桥暮雨、十里银湖、"小桥流水人家"等移步换景的视觉效果,使运河成为一条雅俗共赏的夜游路线。

Figure 2-2   The lighting upgrading of the canal

图 2-2   运河亮化提升工程

In the lightening project, the 10 city entrances mentioned above referred to the Shanghai-Hangzhou-Ningbo Pengbu entrance, Shanghai-Hangzhou-Ningbo Desheng entrance, Beltway Nanzhuangdou entrance, Beltway Hangzhou north entrance, Beltway Hangzhou south entrance, Beltway Liuxia entrance, airport highway Xixing entrance, airport highway main entrance, east railway station and the city railway station. They are all important gateways to Hangzhou. This work had lit the city entrances and surrounding structures to improve functional lighting and nightscape quality.

亮化工程中,上文提到的 10 个入城口,指的是沪杭甬彭埠入口、沪杭甬德胜入口、绕城南庄兜入口、绕城杭州北入口、绕城杭州南入口、绕城留下入口、机场公路西兴入口、机场公路主线入口、火车东站和城站火车站,都是进入杭州的重要门户。此次工作对城口及周边建筑的景观实施了亮化,提升了功能性照明和夜环境品质。

What's more, the project mainly focused on West Lake Circuit Road, important commercial city streets, and backbone highways in the city, while about 40 roads in Hangzhou also followed to start the lighting upgrading work.

此外,以环西湖道路、城市重要商业街、城市骨干高架轴为重点,杭州约 40 条道路也相继启动沿线亮化提升工作。

Here comes the third example. It is no doubt that the acceleration of the internalization process of Hangzhou or even Zhejiang Province requires a complete equipment of foreign language services. In order to make the foreign guests' stay in Hangzhou during the G20 Summit convenient, Hangzhou Bus Group, through the processing of details such as translation and recording, took the lead to equip the bus and subway with station broadcasting in both Mandarin and English during the G20 Summit and Post-G20 Era. English station broadcasting has been put into use since July 2016 in the subways and the main routes in the city center. The new English recordings for station announcement in subways, compared to the old version, are clearly more original in accent and more accurate in expressions.

以下为第三个例子。毋庸置疑,加速杭州乃至浙江的国际化进程,少不了外语服务的配套跟进。为了方便 G20 期间来杭的外宾出行,杭州公交集团经过对翻译和录制等细节的处理,牵头为 G20 峰会和后峰会时代的公交和地铁配备了普通话加英语的双语报站服务。地铁和主城区的主要道路公交英语报站已于 2016 年 7 月投入使用。新的地铁英语报站的录音和老版的录音相比,口音更为纯正,表达更为准确。

Public transportation is the main way of people's daily travel, and also an important platform for cultural exchanges between people. The addition of

English station broadcasting systems is standard equipment for international cities. At the same time, Hangzhou is a tourism destination. In order to make Hangzhou much more international, public transportation should be promoted as a primary window for Hangzhou's image.

公共交通是人们日常出行的主要方式，也是人们文化交流的重要平台，加入英语报站是国际化都市的标配。同时，杭州是一个旅游城市，为了让杭州旅游走向世界，公共交通应提升品质，成为展示杭州形象的首要窗口。

In the past, if you took a look at the streets of Hangzhou, you would find that the content and styles of many road sign were not unified or even had errors. However, back in the summer of 2015, Hangzhou launched *International Design Guide for Hangzhou Urban Sign System*. According to this guide, the road name signs of the first 46 major roads in Hangzhou had already become "internationalized" by the end of April in 2016.

若是以前，到杭州的街头仔细看看，会发现有不少路名标识的内容和样式不统一，甚至有些标识存在错误。但乘着峰会筹备的东风，杭州早在 2015 年夏就出台了《杭州城市标识系统国际化设计导引》。以此为引导，2016 年 4 月底，杭州首批 46 条主要道路的路名标识变得"国际化"。

It is very important to translate road names appropriately to make foreigners understand clearly. As to the Chinese-English translation for road names, Hangzhou has already established a uniform standard: using Pinyin for specific place names and English for common parts known over the world. As for the general information, the first letter is supposed to be uppercase and the rest lowercase.

要让外国友人看明白，路名翻译就很重要。路名牌的英译，杭州已经制定了统一的标准：专名部分使用汉语拼音，通用部分用英语。一般信息的首字母大写，其余小写。

Specification is the foundation and "internationalization" is the goal. The 46 roads' reconstruction was only the first step and it had leaded the coordination of the relevant departments to refine and concrete the standards of sign systems of all industries.

规范是基础，"国际化"是目标。46 条道路标识的改造只是第一步，由此引出了后续各相关部门的协调，以促进各行业标识系统的标准制定和逐步细化、具象化。

The last example is that we found many websites about Hangzhou and Zhejiang Province received high attention because of the Summit, which also contributed to the relevant departments to create or improve the bilingual or multilingual websites. On September 27, 2016, media reporters, tourists both in and out of the province, and representatives of international friends gathered in the West Lake Museum to witness the launching of Zhejiang Tourism's foreign languages website. At the same time, the first event of its foreign languages website "Cross the Ocean to See You-the Post-G20 West Lake Tours for International

Figure 2-3   Translation of Road Names

图 2-3   杭州路牌翻译

Friends" also formally started recruiting international experience staff for West Lake on the website. The foreign languages website of Zhejiang Tourism is a crucial window for our province's tourism to show its image outside Zhejiang Province or even abroad.

最后一个例子是,关于杭州和浙江省的多个网站因为峰会的关系受到了高度关注,而这也促使相关单位创建和完善网站的双语化或多语化进程。2016 年 9 月 27 日,来自省内外的媒体记者、旅游达人和国际友人代表欢聚西湖博物馆,共同见证浙江旅游外文网站正式上线。与此同时,外文网站首次活动——"'漂洋过海来看你'后 G20 时代国际友人寻迹西湖活动"在浙江旅游外文网站正式启动,招募西湖国际体验师。浙江旅游外文网站是我省旅游展示对外形象、进行国际宣传的重要窗口之一。

Besides, during the Summit, the foreign languages website of Zhejiang Tourism Bureau had launched two versions: English and Japanese. It primarily focused on the European and American visitors while covering other areas with the first principle to meet tourists' needs. The website aims to show friendly user interface, rich content, outstanding themes and optimized functions to the greatest extent. According to the introduction by relevant personnel of E-government office, during the Summit, page views of the government portal website "HANGZHOU. GOV. CN," the E-government Affairs Network, and other kinds of office business system and static pages have increased many times than before.

除此之外,G20 期间,浙江省旅游局推出的外文网站分为英文版和日文版两个版本。网站在定位上以面向欧美游客为主,兼顾其他区域,以满足游客需求为第一原则,最大限度体现用户界面友好、内容丰富、主题突出、功能完善的门户网站特色。根据电子政务办相关人员介绍,峰会期间,"中国杭州"政府门户网站连同电子政务外网、各类办公业务系统及静态页面的浏览量比以往增加了许多倍。

To draw a conclusion, the G20 Summit mainly affects Hangzhou in three different ways.

总体来说,G20 峰会在杭举办,主要在以下三个方面影响这座城市。

First of all, the G20 Summit helps enhance the international popularity and reputation of Hangzhou. In China, Hangzhou undoubtedly has a high reputation and popularity. However, Hangzhou's popularity is relatively small internationally. People may learn something about Beijing because it is the capital of China, know Shanghai because it is a prosperous metropolis, and hear about Yiwu for it is a world-class small commodity distribution center. However, it seems that people knew little about Hangzhou, which is really unfortunate. The G20 Summit offers Hangzhou an excellent opportunity to promote itself to the world. The G20 leaders gathered in Hangzhou, followed by a large number of journalists, great entrepreneurs and many tourists. After the Summit, Hangzhou has attracted more attention of the world, which has greatly enhanced the visibility of Hangzhou City. The Summit was a complete success, and Hangzhou's reputation has greatly improved.

首先,G20 峰会有助于提升杭州的国际知名度、美誉度。在中国,杭州无疑拥有极高的知名度和美誉度,但在国际上,杭州的知名度相对较小。很多外国人知道北京,中国的首都;知道上海,那是东方国际大都市;知道义乌,那是世界级的小商品集散地。但是,知道杭州的人却不是那么多,这的确是个很大的遗憾。G20 峰会在杭州举办,给了杭州一个极好的机会宣传自己。G20 国家的领导人汇聚杭州,随之而来的是大批媒体人、全球企业家和大量游客。会后,杭州吸引了全世界的目光。G20 峰会使全世界的人关注杭州、了解杭州,必将极大地提升杭州的城市知名度。峰会取得圆满成功,杭州的城市美誉度也大大提升。

Secondly, the G20 Summit helps Hangzhou attract more foreign investment. We must seize the chance of investment to accelerate the transformation of economic development. In the G20 Summit, leaders and entrepreneurs around the world gathered in Hangzhou, and had an intuitive understanding of Hangzhou. This is undoubtedly one of the best opportunities for attracting investment. The Fifth Plenary Session of the Eighth Central Committee of the Communist Party of China (CPC) recently put forward five major development concepts of innovation, coordination, greenness, openness and sharing, and opened a profound transformation in the overall development of the country. Zhejiang Province as well as Hangzhou City needs to seize the rare opportunity of the G20 to actively create an atmosphere of investment, promote economic restructuring and upgrading, and enhance regional development as a whole.

其次,G20 峰会有助于杭州引进外资。加快转变对外经济发展方式,必须抓住招商引资这个关键环节。G20 峰会,世界各国的领导人和企业家莅临杭州,直观地了解杭州,这无疑是一个最好的招商引资机会。不久前召开的十八届五中全会提出创新、协调、绿色、开放、共享五大发展理念,开启了关系国家发展全局的一场深刻变革。开放性的政策理念和主张,体现了战略视野和政治远见。浙江省和杭州市都要抓住 G20 峰会这一难得机遇,积极营造投资氛围,促进经济转型升级和区域统筹发展。

Furthermore, the holding of G20 Summit helps improve the environment and traffic conditions in Hangzhou, and improve the quality of urban life. The G20 Summit is an important international event, and we should strive to show the best and most beautiful side of Hangzhou to the world. Therefore, we must make great efforts to rectify the environment. Besides, in order to ensure the smooth convening of the G20 Summit, the promotion of the construction of roads, airports, subways and other infrastructure is in need. Afterall, the G20 Summit guests only used these infrastructure for a moment, the real benefits go to the citizens of Hangzhou. All these improvements certainly help improve the quality of life in Hangzhou.

再者,举办 G20 峰会有助于改善杭州的环境、交通状况,提升城市生活品质。G20 峰会是重要的国际盛会,我们要努力展现杭州最好、最美的一面,必须下大力气整治环境。此外,为了保障大会顺利召开,推进道路、机场、地铁等基础设施建设也是非常必要的。这些设施,大会来宾使用只是一时,真正的受益人是杭州市民。这些改变必然有助于提升杭州市民的生活品质。

2.1.2 Words, Phrases and Sentences 词汇、短语和例句

the Geneva Conventions《日内瓦公约》

headquarter 总部

internationalized 国际化的

permanent neutral state 永久中立国

entrepreneur 企业家

first-tier city 一线城市

infrastructure 基础设施

premier 总理

financial crisis 金融危机

A Good Host, A Better G20 办好 G20,当好东道主

bicycle availability of the surrounding stops 周边点的车辆空满情况

a city that never sleeps 不夜城

user interface 用户界面

outstanding theme 主题突出

optimized function 功能完善

to the greatest extent 最大限度地

promote economic restructuring and upgrading 促进经济转型升级

(1) With the success of the G20 Summit in 2016, the popularity and influence of Hangzhou have been "vitalized" rapidly. Compared to Geneva and other renowned international "meeting capitals," Hangzhou has both disadvantages and its own unique advantages.

随着 2016 年 G20 峰会的成功举办,杭州的知名度与影响力都迅速"动"起来了。相对于日内瓦等国际知名"会议之都",杭州存在不足也有自己得天独厚的优势。

(2) Among them, public bicycles of Hangzhou had a largest overhaul ever to match with the Summit (completed by the end of 2016). After upgrading of

the public bicycle system, the functions of self-assist search machines had been improved greatly, thus making the operation more convenient.

其中,为助力 G20 峰会,杭州公共自行车迎来了史上的最强升级(于 2016 年底前完成)。升级后,服务点内自助查询机的功能有很大提升,操作起来也更加方便自如。

(3) Another example, in the preparation of the G20 Summit, Hangzhou, for the first time, started the systematic upgrading work of the whole city lighting. It's not only lighting for three core scenic areas of West Lake, the Grand Canal and Qiantang River, but also the "dressing up" for the primary roads and 10 city entrances.

再比如,为了准备 G20 峰会,杭州首次启动全城系统化亮化提升工作,不仅围绕西湖、运河、钱塘江三大核心景区进行景观灯光提升工作,还将对重要道路及 10 个入城口进行亮化"装扮"。

(4) The last example is that we found many websites about Hangzhou and Zhejiang Province received high attention because of the Summit, which also contributed to the relevant departments to create or improve the bilingual or multilingual websites.

最后一个例子是,我们发现关于杭州和浙江省的多个网站因为峰会的关系受到了高度关注,而这也促使相关单位创建和完善网站的双语化或多语化进程。

2.1.3 Messages from Foreign Guests 外宾留言

2.1.3.1 Mr. Muhammad Shimshak, Vice-premier of Turkey
土耳其副总理穆罕穆德·希姆谢克

"China is the most significant contributor to the world economic development and the engine of the world economy," he said. Despite the fact that the global financial crisis has been gone for more than eight years, the current world economy is still in trouble. The global economic recovery is weak, but China's economy has a strong performance. He believes that the current world economic situation would be weaker without China's economic eye-catching performance. He hoped that the world economy could set sail again through the implementation of the Hangzhou Action Plan. He also spoke highly of the organization of the G20 Hangzhou Summit.

希姆谢克表示,当前中国是对世界经济发展贡献最大的国家,是世界经济的引擎。尽管全球金融危机已过去八年多,但当前世界经济依然存在困境,复苏乏力,而中国是为数不多的几个亮点之一。他认为,如果不是中国经济的抢眼表现,当前世界经济的处境会更加困难。他希望通过实施本次峰会的"杭州行动计划",世界经济能够再次起航。希姆谢克还对 G20 杭州峰会的组织工作给予了高度评价。

2.1.3.2 Mr. Michel Temer, President of Brazil
巴西总统米歇尔·特梅尔

During his visit, he said that China's confidence in its economy set an example to the rest of the world. The G20 Hangzhou Summit also provides an opportunity for the rest to learn from Chinese experience which is significant to both Brazil and other countries in the world. "I think there are more countries that want to join the G20." He said, "We are all developing countries and getting together can promote the common development of all the countries."

特梅尔在访问中谈到,中国经济对世界最大的榜样作用在于对自身经济的信心。中国的经验对于巴西及其他国家都有极大的意义。而 G20 杭州峰会的召开,也给与会各方提供了学习的机会。特梅尔说:"我觉得还有更多的国家想加入二十国集团中,我们都是发展中国家,大家聚在一起有利于共同发展。"

2.1.3.3 Ban Ki-moon, the Eighth Secretary-General of the UN
前联合国秘书长潘基文

Ban Ki-moon, UN Secretary-General, spoke highly of the Chinese leadership in hosting the Hangzhou Summit of the Group of 20 (G20) on promoting green growth and bolstering the presence of developing countries. "I commend China for steering the G20 Summit this year in such a successful way, leading the G20 towards an action agenda that will come in full support of the 2030 Agenda for Sustainable Development and the Paris Agreement on Climate Change." He added, "This is the first time that the G20 leaders are gathering to discuss the Sustainable Development Goals, climate change, and how we will implement them in parallel."

前联合国秘书长潘基文高度称赞中国在筹办 G20 杭州峰会过程中推进了绿色增长,强化了发展中国家的存在感。"我认可中国指引此次 G20 朝着全力支持《2030 可持续发展议程》和《巴黎气候协定》的行动的方向进行,此次峰会取得了重大成功。"他说,"这是二十国集团领导人第一次聚会讨论可持续发展目标和气候变化,以及我们如何平衡实施这些目标。"

2.1.3.4 Mr. Nursultan Abishevich Nazarbayev, President of Kazakhstan
哈萨克斯坦总统努尔苏丹·阿比舍维奇·纳扎尔巴耶夫

Nazarbayev said that as a rotating presidency of the G20 Summit, China is committed to promoting innovation, the new industrial revolution and the digital economy, and Kazakhstan fully supports China's approach. The G20 Summit is now considered to be a mechanism to solve global economic problems, coordinate macroeconomic policies of member countries and reform the world's financial system. The G20 Summit must show the capacity of unity when the uncertainty of the world's geopolitics and international finance is increasing to maintain the stability of the world economy.

纳扎尔巴耶夫表示,作为 G20 峰会轮值主席国,中国致力于推动创新、新工业革命及数字经济,哈萨克斯坦完全支持中方的这一做法。G20 峰会现在被视为解决全球经济问题、协调成员宏观经济政策及改革世界金融体系的最重要机制。由于世界地缘政治和国际金融所面临的不确定性在增加,G20 峰会必须展现团结大国的能力,以确保世界经济稳定。

2.1.3.5 Mr. Abdel Fattah el-Sisi, President of Egypt
埃及总统阿卜杜勒·法塔赫·塞西

"The G20 Hangzhou Summit, themed as building a world economy with innovation, dynamic, cooperation and inclusion, fits the needs of today's world economy. Hangzhou has made huge and creative efforts to the Summit, and I believe that the Summit must be a great success." Sisi also said that Egypt attaches great importance to learning from China's advanced experience in various fields, including the reform of local government administrative capacity and the development of information technology, agricultural technology and so on. He stressed that Egypt is willing to continue to work closely with China in various fields.

"G20 杭州峰会以构建创新、活力、联动、包容的世界经济为主题,契合当今世界经济的需要。杭州为主办此次峰会做出了创造性的巨大努力,相信峰会一定会圆满成功。"塞西还表示,埃及重视学习中国不同领域的先进经验,其中包括地方政府行政管理能力改革及发展信息科技和农业技术等方面的成功做法。他强调,埃及愿继续与中国在各领域展开密切合作。

2.1.3.6 Nelly, from the United States
尼力,来自美国

My first visit to Hangzhou was about five years ago, shortly after we moved to China from Las Vegas. West Lake had already been pointed out to us as a must-see, so we were excited when a work opportunity presented itself.

我第一次到杭州是大约五年前,那时候我们刚从拉斯维加斯搬到中国不久。人们说西湖是到中国必去的景点,所以当一个到杭州工作的机会出现时我们感到很兴奋。

After months of being in Beijing, it was a huge relief to land in Hangzhou, where even the very air smelled fresher. We spent the whole day walking around West Lake, taking a boat ride, and just soaking up the atmosphere. What I remember most about that day, other than the numerous couples dressed in wedding gear posing for photos, was the general feeling of calm and relaxation—meandering through the scenic lake on a lazy boat, sometimes going under bridges and passing the wedding couples in all their finery.

在北京待了几个月之后再到杭州,心情十分舒畅,杭州的空气更清新。我们花了整整一天来游览西湖,乘船,沉醉在西湖的景色之中。那天,令我记忆犹新的,与其说是湖边一对对新人穿着礼服摆出各种姿势拍照,倒不如说是一种平静悠闲的总体感觉——乘船游走在湖面上,穿过座座小桥,分享着新人们的幸福。

I also remember the amazing food, which was more like the American Chinese food we were used to than what we had experienced in Beijing. A visit to Hangzhou during the first difficult months in China gave me hope that things could get better, and they did.

我还记得那些美味的食物,杭州的中国菜比起北京的中国菜来更像是我们习惯的美式中国菜。在杭州的经历让我有信心克服到中国后最难适应的前几个月,让我相信一切都将变好,事实也的确如此。

2.1.3.7 Owen Fishwick, from the United Kingdom
欧文·菲斯维克,来自英国

With its legendary West Lake, classic cuisine and richness in silk, Hangzhou was at the top of my list of places to visit when I arrived in China almost three years ago. And it didn't disappoint me.

因为有久负盛名的西湖、经典美食和华丽的丝绸,在我三年前来到中国时,杭州就位列要游览的主要目的地之中。杭州果然没有让我失望。

Stepping off the carriage at Hangzhou train station for a three-day stay during Spring Festival, I told my taxi driver one of the few Chinese words I knew at the time, "Xihu" (West Lake). He knew exactly where to take me, and within a few short minutes I was standing on the lake's shore, staring across the calm water at the ancient bridges and pagodas in the distance.

春节期间我在杭州游览了三天,在杭州火车站,我用当时所知的不多的几句中文和出租车司机说了"西湖",他便准确地将我送达了目的地。一会儿,我便来到了西湖边,目光越过平静的水面凝视着远处古老的小桥、高塔。

Over the next three days I got a real taste of Chinese culture, history and cuisine. It was the perfect introduction to China for me, and a time that I will remember fondly for many years to come.

在接下来的三天中,我真正体验到了中国文化、历史和美食。杭州将中国文化完美地展示在我眼前,让我久久不能忘怀。

2.1.3.8 Judith, from Singapore
朱迪思,来自新加坡

When I visited the storied West Lake in Hangzhou with my best friend, I really felt like I was touching history and legend. Not only was the supposed site of the legend of Madam White Snake, a story I had heard from my childhood, it was also such a beautiful and poetic landscape that had been described and portrayed by so many artists and writers in Chinese art and literature. But what impressed me the most was what I learned about Su Dongpo, the Song dynasty poet and statesman whose impact on Hangzhou was so great that he is still fondly remembered and celebrated there.

当我和我最好的朋友一起到充满传奇色彩的杭州西湖游览时,我觉得自己仿佛触摸到了那些历史和传说。西湖不但是"白娘子"这一我从小时候就耳熟能详的故事发生的地方,也是一个历来被中国的文人墨客所描绘和歌颂的景点。令我印象最深的是我所了解到的苏东坡的传奇故事。苏东坡是宋代诗人和政治家,他对杭州这座城市影响深远,至今为杭州人所称颂。

I had known of Su Dongpo mainly because of his poetry, but I was impressed that he had been an accomplished statesman too, and that he had had the pedestrian walkway across West Lake built (it still bears his name, Sudi, or Su Causeway today) and that it survives to this day. How many public works have lasted a thousand years? Furthermore, I was very moved by the story of how the people of Hangzhou named Dongpo Pork after him because he had been awarded a large portion of meat and decided to share it with the commoners. Here was a man who left a meaningful legacy behind. Although he lived over a thousand years ago, the memory about him was my strongest impression of Hangzhou.

我知道苏东坡主要是因为他的诗歌,但我很惊讶他也是一位成功的政治家。在他任内,西湖建设了一条穿湖而过的行人通道(这条通道以他的姓命名,称作"苏堤"),并保留至今。试问有多少公共工程能沿用千年呢?此外,还有一个故事让我非常感动。传说曾经苏东坡得到很多肉,他毫不吝啬地拿出来与普通百姓分享,人们为了纪念他便以他的名字命名了一道菜,叫作"东坡肉"。他是个留下了有意义的遗产的人。虽然他生活在1000多年前,但对他的记忆是我对杭州最深的印象。

2.1.4 Extensive Links 拓展链接

2.1.4.1 A brief introduction to Geneva 日内瓦简介

Geneva is the second most populous city in Switzerland (after Zurich) and is the most populous city of Romandy, the French-speaking part of Switzerland.

日内瓦是瑞士人口第二多的城市(仅次于苏黎世),是瑞士法语区罗曼迪人口最多的城市。

Geneva is a global city, a financial center, and a worldwide center for diplomacy due to the presence of numerous international organizations, including the headquarters of many agencies of the United Nations and the Red Cross. Geneva is the city that hosts the largest number of international organizations in the world. It is also the place where the Geneva Conventions, which chiefly concern the treatment of wartime non-combatants and prisoners of war, were signed.

日内瓦是国际化都市、金融中心和外交中心。因为它是许多国际组织的所在地,是联合国许多机构和红十字会的总部。日内瓦是世界上拥有国际组织最多的城市。主要涉及战时非战斗人员和战俘的待遇问题的《日内瓦公约》也在这里签署。

Geneva was ranked as the world's ninth most important financial center for competitiveness by the Global Financial Centers Index, ahead of Frankfurt, and third in Europe behind London and Zurich. A 2009 survey by Mercer found that Geneva has the third-highest quality of life of any city in the world. It has been referred to as the world's most compact metropolis and the "Peace Capital." In 2009 and 2011, Geneva was ranked as, respectively, the fourth and fifth most expensive city in the world.

Figure 2-4　Geneva

图 2-4　日内瓦

日内瓦被全球金融中心指数列为世界第九大最富竞争力的金融中心,位于法兰克福之前、伦敦和苏黎世之后,高居欧洲第三位。美世咨询公司 2009 年的一项调查发现,日内瓦的生活质量高居全球第三。这个城市被称为世界上最小的大都市和"和平之都"。2009 年和 2011 年,日内瓦在世界生活成本最高的城市排名中分别被列世界第四、第五位。

2.1.4.2 A brief introduction to the Geneva Conventions
《日内瓦公约》简介

The Geneva Conventions comprise four treaties, and three additional protocols, that establish the standards of international law for the humanitarian treatment in war. The singular term Geneva Convention usually denotes the agreements of 1949, negotiated in the aftermath of the Second World War (1939—1945), which updated the terms of the first three treaties (1864, 1906, 1929), and added a fourth. The Geneva Conventions extensively define the basic rights of wartime prisoners (civilians and military personnel), establish protections for the wounded and sick, and establish protections for the civilians in and around a war-zone. The treaties of 1949 were ratified, in whole or with reservations, by 196 countries. Moreover, the Geneva Conventions also define the rights and protections afforded to non-combatants, yet, because the Geneva Conventions are about people in war, the articles do not address warfare proper—the use of weapons of war—which is the subject of the Hague

Conventions (First Hague Conference, 1899; Second Hague Conference, 1907), and the bio-chemical warfare Geneva Protocol (Protocol for the Prohibition of the Use in War of Asphyxiating, Poisonous or other Gases, and of Bacteriological Methods of Warfare, 1925).

《日内瓦公约》包括四项条约和三项附加议定书,确立了战争中人道主义待遇的国际法标准。单一名词"日内瓦公约"通常表示在第二次世界大战(1939—1945 年)之后通过谈判达成的 1949 年协定,该协定更新了前三项条约(1864 年,1906 年,1929 年)的条款,并增加了第四项。《日内瓦公约》界定了战时囚犯(包括平民和军事人员)的基本权利、为伤病者提供保护,并为战区及战区周围的平民建立了保护。1949 年的条约得到 196 个国家的全面或部分接受。此外,《日内瓦公约》还界定了给予非战斗人员的权利和保护。但是由于《日内瓦公约》是关于战争中的人的公约,这些条款没能对战争中武器的使用做出制约——这是《海牙公约》(第一次海牙会议,1899 年;第二次海牙会议,1907 年)和生物化学战《日内瓦议定书》(《禁止在战争中使用窒息性、毒性或其他气体和细菌作战方法的议定书》,1925 年)所讨论的主题。

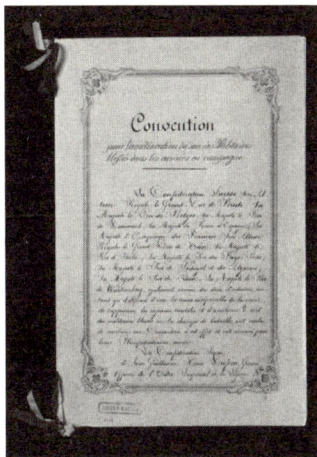

Figure 2-5   the Geneva Conventions
图 2-5   《日内瓦公约》

2.2 Preparation Work of Conferences
会议筹备工作

2.2.1 Brief Introduction 简介

Preparation of LICs is a practical project quite worthy of study and research generally because of numerous delegations from all over the world, the relatively complex conference programs and other related work. Taking the G20 Summit as an example, this section firstly makes a brief introduction to the preparatory work under the guide of the presidency taskforce including conference programs, conference accommodation and venues, accreditation, contacts, international travel and domestic transport, media, security and health care, etc. Secondly, words, phrases and sentences quite useful in the case of LICs are selected and then relevant situational practice is designed to nurture the application ability. In addition, two new modules, interviews with conference staff and extensive links, are added to this section.

大型国际会议的筹备,往往因世界各地的代表团众多,并且会议日程和其他会务工作较为复杂,成为一个非常值得学习和研究的实践课题。本小节以 G20峰会为例,首先简单介绍一下在峰会筹备办指导下的,包括会议日程、会议住宿与会场、注册工作、联络人员、国际旅程与国内交通、媒体、安保与医疗等的准备工作,然后筛选其中较为实用的词汇、短语和例句,并且设计相关情景演练以培养应用能力。另外,本小节新添了工作人员访谈和拓展链接两个模块。

2.2.1.1 Conference programs 会议日程

Conference programs allocate each activity (including ritual and supportive activities) to the time unit. Conferences lasting one day (one day = two time units) or more should have conference programs, while programs of LICs tend to be more complicated and important. Given that many readers are confused about the two concepts, conference programs and conference agenda, here it is made clear that conference programs include the conference agenda (i. e. , the overall arrangements for the activity order related to the meeting topics) and other rituals or supportive activities during the conference. Therefore, the concept of conference programs is larger than that of the conference agenda.

会议日程是将各项会议活动(包括仪式性、辅助性活动)落实到单位时间,凡会期满一天及以上(即两个单位时间)的会议都应当制订会议日程,而大型国际会议的日程则更为复杂重要。鉴于许多读者都会混淆会议日程和会议议程两个概念,这里明确指出会议日程包括会议议程(即整个会议议题性活动顺序的总体安排)和会议期间的仪式性、辅助性的活动。因此,会议日程的概念大于会议议程。

For most citizens, the 2016 G20 Hangzhou Summit probably only refers to the Leaders' Summit on September 4 to 5. However, despite the fact that the two-day Leaders' Summit is of the highest specification during the whole G20, it is still only one of the conference programs. From the micro perspective, the 2016 G20 Hangzhou Summit also includes the Finance and Central Bank Deputies Meeting, the fourth Sherpa Meeting and other rituals or supportive activities such as spouse activities, foreign ministers' activities and finance ministers' activities. While from a macro perspective, from the first Finance and

Central Bank Deputies Meeting in Sanya in December, 2015 to the fifth Sherpa Meeting in Wuhan in October, 2016, China has written a great chapter once the whole year is considered as a summit year.

对于许多老百姓来说,2016 年 G20 杭州峰会也许只是指 9 月 4 日—5 日的领导人峰会。然而,两天的领导人峰会虽是整个峰会中规格最高的一场会议,但也只是会议日程中的一项。从微观角度来讲,2016 年 G20 杭州峰会还包括财政副手会议、第四次协调人会议,以及配偶活动、外交部部长活动和财长活动等仪式性、辅助性活动。而从宏观角度来讲,从 2015 年 12 月三亚第一次财政副手会议开始至 2016 年 10 月武汉第五次协调人会议,中国可以说谱写了一个峰会年。

As the Leaders' Summit is of the highest specification hosted in Chinese history, the G20 gathered heads and dignitaries of G20 members and many guest countries as well as heads of the international organizations. The participating group, including these heads and dignitaries along with their entourage and media staff, was huge and complicated. The successful host of this Summit will affect the global economic governance order for the foreseeable future.

作为中国历史上主办的规格最高的国家领导人峰会,G20 聚集了二十国集团和多个嘉宾国国家元首、政要,国际组织负责人参会。参加峰会的各国元首、政要及随行人员、媒体记者等人员庞大而复杂。会议的成功主办,将影响今后一个时期的全球经济治理秩序。

During the Summit, regardless of the Leaders' Summit, the welcome dinner or the West Lake gala, the careful deployment and repeated practice behind the scenes constituted a large ordeal. Supportive activities over the same period, such as partner dialogues, spouse activities, theme meetings had been also under exclusive management of a specific department. At the same time, the informal meeting of Brics leaders, G20 Sherpa Meeting, Finance and Central Back Deputies Meeting and B20 were held. From the welcome and seeing-off to the agenda, entertaining dinners and performances, every conference program requires methodical processes. Among them, the protocol reception of state-level heads is essentially a task calling for special rules, rigorous procedures and precision. "Foreign affairs are never small issues," from the big venue arrangement to the small tableware decoration, everything calls for rigorous procedures and special rules in accordance to "details as the key" without even the smallest mistake.

峰会期间,除了举办的国家领导人会议,欢迎晚宴、文艺演出都经过精心部署和多次演练,这都是重大考验。同期举办的诸如伙伴对话会、配偶活动、主题边会等峰会配套活动也都实行了专属部门责任制。金砖国家领导人非正式会晤、G20协调人会议、财政副手会议及工商峰会等也同期举行。从迎送开始,到议程,再到宴请和演出,每一项日程都要求有条不紊地进行。其中,元首级礼宾接待更是一项特别讲规矩、讲程序、重严谨的工作。"外事无小事",大到场馆安排,小到餐具摆设,凡事都要讲程序、讲规矩,做到"细节为王",容不得半点闪失。

2.2.1.2 Conference accommodation and venues 会议住宿和会场

From the perspective of conference accommodation and venues, the preparatory work of LICs also needs quite a long time to fulfill. Take the G20 Hangzhou Summit as an example, firstly, the taskforce would send professionals to study the catering, accommodation, venues, tours, entertainment and other related aspects of Hangzhou on the spot, on which the draft of the accommodation and venues was based. Secondly, the scale and level of the G20 Summit put forward an unprecedented test for the hotels' reception and the venues' preparation in Hangzhou. As to almost all the LICs, in terms of foreign guests, especially high-level foreign guests, the services of protocol, welcome and public relations assigned to specific personnel in the airport or station, embody high demands and requirements on foreign languages. Except from the staff in charge of reception for LICs, the provincial youth league and the municipal youth league under CCP are usually responsible to recruit a large number of volunteers with comprehensive qualities, especially excellent cross-cultural communication quality. As to the confirmation of hotel room floors and room numbers along with meal time, eating standards and special guests (Muslims), inquiries in advance about any special needs are necessary. Thirdly, the draft of bilingual signs in venues needs to be drawn and submitted for approval in advance. Personnel need to be assigned to follow up the preparatory situation of lighting, sound, tea and other goods.

从会议住宿和会场的角度来谈,其筹备工作也需要预留相当长的一段时间来展开。以G20杭州峰会为例,首先,筹备办会派专人实地考察杭州的吃、住、会议场地、游、娱乐等相关方面的情况,并在此基础上草拟会议住宿和会场的预案。其次,峰会的规模和级别,对杭城酒店的会议接待工作和会场的准备工作来说,可谓是一次史无前例的考验。对于大型国际会议来说,在对待外宾,特别是高规格外宾的情况下,机场或车站的礼仪、接站、公关等服务都由专人负责,对外语的需求和要求都很大。除了负责接待工作的工作人员之外,团省委及团市委通常负责牵头配备大量综合素质特别是跨文化交流素质良好的志愿者。关于入住房间楼层及房间号确认,还有用餐时间、用餐标准及特殊客人(穆斯林)的确认,需提前询问是否有特殊要求。再次,各个会场的双语指示牌方案要求提前制定和报批,并由专人到会议室负责和跟进灯光、音响、茶饮及其他会议用品的准备情况。

The 2016 G20 Chinese Presidency Taskforce designated 26 hotels for G20 Delegations, and had already contacted with each delegation through the necessary protocols to recommend a specific hotel within the list for their leaders before the G20 Hangzhou Summit. All the designated hotels met the logistic and security requirements of the 2016 G20 Chinese Presidency Taskforce, and hotels offered standard meeting services, such as shuttle buses and medical center, etc. Under the instruction from China's Ministry of Foreign Affairs, hotel information had been sent in advance via e-mail to the Delegation Contact Officer (DCO) or the Delegation Accreditation Officer (DAO). At the same time, the Chinese Presidency Taskforce appointed a Liaison Officer (LO) to each delegation so that inquiries related to accommodation can be discussed through the designated LO.

2016 年 G20 中国筹备办为峰会代表团官方指定了 26 家酒店,并且通过各国礼宾司渠道为特定名单中的领导人推荐具体的一家酒店。所有指定的酒店都满足了 2016 年 G20 中国筹备办关于后勤和安保方面的要求。酒店会提供诸如班车和医疗点等在内的标准化服务。酒店信息由中国外交部牵头,提前通过邮件发放给各代表团的联络官或注册官。同时,中方为各代表团任命相应的中方联络官,各代表团可以联系中方联络官来沟通住宿方面的要求。

Since we have already introduced the main venue of the G20 in the third section of Chapter 1, here we are wondering what kind of preparatory work we had done in the main venue as well as the session venues. Because English was the official language of the G20 Hangzhou Summit, during the summit, foreign delegations were kindly requested to bring their own simultaneous interpreters as the host country only provided simultaneous interpretation between Chinese and English. The 2016 G20 Chinese Presidency Taskforce provided technical equipment upon request, such as the booths for simultaneous interpretation. Information Desks were operating during the Summit both at HIEC, the main venue, and the session venues such as Intercontinental Hotel, Dragon Hotel, etc. , in order to facilitate meeting logistics and to provide delegates with information and assistance.

我们在 1.3 中已经介绍了主会场的概况,那么在主会场和分会场主要有哪些筹备工作要开展呢？由于英语是 G20 杭州峰会的官方语言,在杭州峰会期间,欢迎外方代表团携带自己的同声传译员,主办国家只提供中英文之间的同声传译服务。2016 年 G20 峰会中国筹备办在外方要求的情况下提供同传箱等技术设备。主会场杭州国博中心,以及其他诸如洲际酒店、黄龙饭店等分会场的国际服务台在峰会期间 24 小时运营,以保障会议后勤,为代表提供信息和帮助。

Figure 2-6　Information Desk during the Summit
图 2-6　峰会期间的咨询台图片

2. 2. 1. 3 Conference accreditation 会议注册

From the perspective of LICs' accreditation, the accreditation aims to ensure every delegate's identity verification to participate in meetings and activities as well as their secure entry into the security venue/area. In a LIC, an accreditation pass/badge normally contains the individual's photo, name and country/organization and must be worn at all times while within designated access-controlled areas. In some cases, accreditation passes/badges are even strictly non-transferable.

从大型国际会议注册的角度来讲,注册是为了确保参加会议和活动的所有代表通过身份验证并能安全地进入安保会场/区域。在一场大型国际会议里,一张经过注册拿到的通行卡/代表证上一般包含个人的照片、姓名和国家/组织,在指定的通行限定区必须佩戴才能进出。在某些情况下,经注册拿到的通行卡/代表证是不能相互转让的。

As to G20, all delegates attending G20 Communique drafting meetings and the Summit must be accredited by the Taskforce via the secure online accreditation portal which had been opened for a certain period. No extensions were declared to be made to this deadline. It was important that delegates register for accreditation via the online accreditation portal as early as possible and then apply for their visas if necessary. All delegations were kindly requested to nominate a Delegation Accreditation Officer (DAO), who was responsible for online registration of ALL members in his/her delegation, badge collection in Hangzhou G20 Accreditation Center and badge distribution to their delegates.

对于 G20 峰会来说，所有参加 G20 公报决策会议和领导人峰会的代表必须通过筹备办的注册平台安全地在网上注册。注册平台在峰会前指定的一段时间开放，不允许延期开放。因此，对于代表们来说，尽早在网上注册平台完成注册，以便申请签证，显得至关重要。所有代表团要求任命一个注册官，其职责是完成该代表团所有代表的网上注册，到杭州 G20 注册中心现场领取参会证件，以及将证件分发给代表们。

2.2.1.4 Conference contacts 会议联络人员

From the perspective of contacts, LICs generally need specific staff for contacts between the host and guests. Like the G20 Summit, Chinese Presidency Taskforce assigned Liaison Officers (LOs) to the following categories of people: Leaders and IO Heads, Spouses of Leaders or IO heads, Sherpa, Finance Deputies and Media Chiefs. The LOs served as point of contact on issues regarding administration and logistics and should be available to facilitate matters prior to the arrivals of the respective leaders, spouses, sherpa or finance deputies.

从联络人员的角度来讲，国际大型会议通常需要指派专人作为主办方和嘉宾团之间的联系纽带。例如，G20 峰会中国筹备办向以下多类人员指派了相应的联络官：国家领导人和国家组织团长、领导人和国际组织团长的配偶、协调人、财政副手和媒体团负责人。联络官负责行政和后勤两方面事宜的沟通协调，并且要在领导人及其配偶、协调人和财政副手抵达前处理好这些事宜。

Each delegation is required to appoint a primary Delegation Contact Officer (DCO). The DCO should accompany their Delegation during the Summit and be available as point of contact regarding any logistic or administrative matter. The

DCO's duties include：

每个参会代表团可以任命一位主联络官。联络官应该在峰会期间陪同本团代表，并且当有后勤和行政事务需要沟通的时候应该在场。参会代表团联络官的具体职责包括：

• To be constantly in touch with the 2016 G20 Chinese Presidency Taskforce during the meetings

和 2016 年 G20 中国筹备办在会议期间保持紧密联系

• To be constantly in touch with LOs

和联络员保持密切联系

• To pick up and distribute meeting kits to members of his/her delegation

领取会议装备并分发给他/她的代表团所有代表

• To pick up invitations for all delegates

领取本团所有代表参加各类活动的邀请函

• To submit bookings (if any) for bilateral meeting rooms

递交双边会议室的预订（如有的话）

2.2.1.5 International travel and domestic transport 国际旅程和国内交通

(1) Visa

Delegates attending LICs out of their home countries are usually concerned about their visas before the conference. For the List of Agreements on Mutual Visa Exemption between the People's Republic of China and foreign countries, please refer to the Mutual Visa Exemption List located on the right column of http://cs. mfa. gov. cn/wgrlh/. Except these listed countries, generally speaking, all other delegates from the LICs' member countries, guest countries or international organizations need valid visas or permits to enter China. LICs' delegates who are not exempted from visa should include the invitation/confirmation letter in their visa application, and are strongly advised to apply early from the Embassies, Consulates, or other visa-issuing authorities of the People's Republic of China accredited to or stationed in the respective member countries. For further inquiries about visa and entry requirements, one may contact a person in charge via a designated e-mail authorized by the LIC. All foreign citizens entering the People's Republic of China are required to undergo a customs inspection.

参加国外举办的大型国际会议的代表参会前都要考虑签证问题。中华人民共和国和其他国家的互免签证名单,请参见网址 http://cs.mfa.gov.cn/wgrlh/ 中右栏的互免签证名单。除了这些国家之外,通常,大型国际会议的成员、嘉宾或国际组织的所有代表都需要有效的签证或许可证方可进入中国境内。无免签资格的代表应提前进行签证申请并附邀请函或确认函。建议各代表到所在国的中国大使馆、领事馆或其他中华人民共和国认可的签证机构办理签证。如需进一步咨询签证和入境要求的相关事宜,可联系由此大型国际会议官方授权的邮箱。所有进入中华人民共和国的外国公民都需要接受海关检查。

Customs declarations are required by China's regulations to be filled out by delegates who bring in cash in excess of USD 5,000 (or its equivalent in another currency) or RMB 20,000 or articles that are subject to customs clearance.

根据中国的规定,在报关时,如有与会代表携带的现金超过 5000 美元(或等值的他国货币)或 20000 元人民币或者携带了一些需要清关的物品的话,那么就需要其填写报关单。

(2)Baggage and item restrictions 行李和条款限制

Given that airlines strictly enforce baggage size and weight limitations, delegates are requested to familiarize themselves with their airline luggage weight and carry-on baggage restrictions prior to traveling in order to avoid extra fees or complications. Inside the check-in area, the delegates can use the baggage packing service. In addition, for the sake of airline security, some articles and substances must not be carried aboard. The amount of liquid in hand luggage may also be restricted.

鉴于航空公司严格执行行李尺寸和重量限制,请与会代表在旅行前熟悉自己的航空行李重量及航空公司对随身行李的限制,以避免产生额外费用或其他不必要的麻烦。代表们可以在办理登机手续的地方使用行李打包服务。此外,为了飞行安全,不得携带违禁物品登机。手提行李中的液体量也受到严格限制。

(3)Airport arrivals and departures 机场抵离

Hangzhou Xiaoshan International Airport (LATA: HGH) is the only international airport serving Hangzhou. There are three terminals at the airport. Terminal 1 and Terminal 3, serving domestic flights, are linked by a walkway. Terminal 2, serving international flights, is about 500 meters' walk from Terminal 1. It is important that delegations should be aware of which terminal they are using and include that information in the communication with their LOs or the conference committee.

杭州萧山国际机场(国际代码:HGH)是目前杭州唯一的国际机场。萧山机场截至目前共有三个航站楼。第一和第三航站楼由一个走廊连接,主要服务于国内航线。第二航站楼主要服务于国际航线,距离第一航站楼 500 米。对于与会代表团而言,在与联络员或组委会沟通时了解清楚航站楼相关信息十分重要。

As to G20, transportation services were provided for the following: leaders and heads of international organizations, spouses, all accredited delegates, and all accredited media members.

就 G20 峰会来说,中方为国际机构的负责人及其配偶、所有取得认证的与会代表、所有取得认证的媒体记者提供交通服务。

A limited number of dedicated car-with-driver services were available to all delegations for use for official G20 business only. Shuttle bus services were provided for delegates in Hangzhou. The schedule of shuttle buses would be available at the G20 Information Desks at the meeting venues. Buses would not depart without even one passenger on board.

组委会向所有代表团提供专车服务,数量有限的专车仅用于官方 G20 业务。组委会为来杭代表提供班车服务,班车时刻表可在会场的 G20 信息服务台获取。在没有乘客的情况下,班车不会离开。

(4)Public transport and taxi 公共交通和出租车

If a LIC is held in a city with fully-equipped public transportation and taxis, delegates are highly recommended to use licensed taxis for transportation. Additional information regarding transportation facilities and taxi services are usually available at the Information Desks at the meeting venues of the LIC, and at the reception desks of the designated hotels.

如果一个大型国际会议在一个公共交通和出租车配备良好的城市举办,我们也推荐与会代表乘坐正规的出租车出行。更多关于交通设施和出租车服务的信息可在大型国际会议会场的信息服务台获取,或向指定下榻酒店的服务台咨询。

(5) Rental vehicles 租车

For most LICs, rental vehicles can be applied in many places except that in the designated area, they need to be accredited or even totally banned. While as to G20, rental vehicles must be accredited to enter the Hangzhou International Expo Center. Accreditation requests were allowed for sedan cars, minivans and vans only. Drivers of these vehicles should be accredited as well. Delegates who required handicap-accessible transportation should notify the 2016 G20 Chinese Presidency Taskforce prior to the beginning of G20 Hangzhou Summit by sending a brief description of their needs to the designated Liaison Officers no later than the deadline.

对于多数大型国际会议来说,租赁车辆可以在许多地方使用,但在指定地区,租赁车辆需要认证才能通行,甚至不能通行。就 G20 峰会来说,租赁车辆必须经过认证才能进入杭州国际博览中心。组委会仅受理轿车、小型货车和厢式车的认证申请,且这些车辆的驾驶人员也需要进行申请。需要无障碍交通设施的代表应在 G20 杭州峰会开始前通知 2016 年 G20 峰会筹备办,并在截止日期前向指定的联络官发送简要说明。

2.2.1.6 Media 媒体

Generally speaking, journalists who wish to attend LICs are required to have invitation letters or register on the designated website. Accredited journalists will be notified to pick up their credentials at a designated place by presenting valid ID and letter of confirmation from their media organizations. Normally, only accredited media representatives can use shuttle buses provided by the organization committee.

一般来说,想要参加大型国际会议的记者必须收到会议邀请函或在指定的网站上进行注册。注册参会的记者将会收到通知,通过提供有效身份证明和其媒体组织给的确认函,在指定地点领取认证书。通常,只有经认证的媒体代表才能使用组委会提供的班车。

During the Hangzhou Summit, the Media Center was established in Block 5 on the ground floor of Hangzhou International Expo Center to facilitate the work of domestic and foreign journalists accredited to cover G20 Hangzhou Summit events. In terms of facilities and functions, the Media Center comprised security checks, check points, comprehensive service desks, public media working area, media booths, public signal and satellite transmission service, television studios, live stand-up positions, press conference halls and briefing rooms, lounge, cultural exhibition and experience area, media assembly point, praying and meditation room, as well as a catering area.

G20 峰会召开期间,媒体中心就设在杭州国际博览中心一楼 5 区。来自国内外的媒体记者可以在这里报道 G20 峰会的各项活动。在设施和功能方面,媒体中心设有安检处、检录处、综合服务台、公共媒体工作区、媒体展位、公共信号和卫星传输服务、电视演播室、现场直播区、新闻发布会厅和简报室、休息室、文化展览和体验区、媒体集中区、祈祷和冥想室、餐饮区。

If the LICs are hosted by the government, accredited journalists bringing professional reporting equipment into China are required to go through necessary customs procedures according to relevant regulations of the General Administration of Customs of the People's Republic of China. The Media Center staff stands ready to assist the journalists in the customs clearance procedures. All equipment should be shipped out of China when the event ends.

如果是政府主办的大型国际会议，按照中华人民共和国海关总署的有关规定，经认可的媒体记者将专业报道设备带入中国境内需办理必要的通关手续。媒体中心工作人员随时待命准备协助国外记者办理清关手续。所有设备应在活动结束时运出中国。

Figure 2-7   The Media Center during the Summit

图 2-7   G20 峰会期间媒体中心工作现场

In the Hangzhou Summit, five hotels in the vicinity of the main venue had been recommended to accredited journalists for their convenience and diversified needs of accommodation, which altogether had more than 2,500 rooms. In these hotels, there were broadband access and multilingual volunteers to facilitate the stay and work of accredited journalists. Public photos taken during the the G20 Hangzhou Summit were uploaded and displayed on the Media Center official website for free downloading. Major activities during the G20 Hangzhou Summit were broadcast live at the Media Center. Host broadcasters provided audio and video download of these activities and satellite transmission services for other media organizations. Media inquiries may be directed to designated e-mail-box on the Media Center official website.

在杭州峰会期间,组委会向取得认证的记者推荐了在主会场附近的五家酒店,为其提供住宿便利,满足其多样化的住宿需求。五家酒店共有超过 2500 间客房可供使用。这些酒店实现宽带全覆盖,并有会多种多语言的志愿者待命,为记者朋友们的工作和生活提供便利。G20 杭州峰会期间拍摄的公开照片上传并展示在媒体中心官方网站上,供免费下载。G20 杭州峰会期间的主要活动能在媒体中心现场直播。主播能为媒体提供这些活动的音频和视频下载及卫星传输服务。媒体的需求可通过媒体中心网站里的指定邮箱进行反馈。

2.2.1.7 Security and health services 安保和医疗

It is absolutely necessary for LICs to have certain security agencies designated for maintaining the smooth progress of all meetings. As to a political LIC like G20, governmental police along with other national security agencies were in charge of the security of the G20 Hangzhou Summit. Apart from ensuring the secure and smooth proceedings of all G20 Hangzhou Summit events, the national security agencies provided protection service to G20 Leaders, Heads of International Organizations, Spouses, and Accompanying Officials above Ministerial level throughout their stay in China. Chinese Police carried out threat assessments of Leaders' Meeting events and other protectees' participation, and accordingly implemented security measures related to personal protection, residential protection, venue protection and route protection. Before the Summit, Chinese Police kindly requested countries to inform of any potential threats for more comprehensive assessments and more targeted protection arrangements.

为了保证所有会议平稳进行,大型国际会议当然需要特定的安保机构。如果是政治性的大型国际会议,比如 G20 峰会,警方与其他国家安全机构一起负责 G20 杭州峰会的安全。除了确保 G20 杭州峰会的所有活动安全和顺利进行外,中国国家安全机构还将为 G20 成员国领导人及其配偶、国际组织负责人及其配偶,以及部长级以上随行官员提供安保服务。中国警方对领导人及其他受保护人员参与的活动进行威胁评估,并实施相应的个人保卫、驻地保护、场馆安保和路线保护。在峰会举办前,中国警方就恳请各国通报任何潜在威胁以便警方更全面评估安全形势和更有针对性的安排保卫任务。

Chinese Police had the obligation to ensure the safety of G20 Leaders while in China. The Leaders' Personal Protection Officers were expected to cooperate with and inform Chinese Police of any off-schedule activity. Where there were any security problems, the Leaders' Personal Protection Officers were asked to turn to Chinese Police for solutions.

中国警方对于确保 G20 与会领导人的安全义不容辞。峰会领导人安全保卫办公室将会与警方通力合作,并通报一切计划外的活动安排。如有任何安全问题,峰会领导人安全保卫办公室都可向警方寻求帮助。

In terms of health care, lots of personnel and money are invested into a LIC. Delegates are usually provided with free basic medical services, first aid and transfer services for emergency cases by medical clinics at meeting venues during meeting hours, and at designated hotels. Medical practitioners are assigned to each delegation for some high-level LICs.

在医疗方面,一场大型国际会议需要大量的人力和财力的投入。在会议期间,代表们通常可在会场及指定酒店中享受免费的基本医疗服务、急救,以及紧急状况下的医疗运送服务。对于一些高规格的国际会议来说,每个代表团都将配备医疗服务人员。

However, we should note that in LICs, the medical clinics at meeting venues and designated hotels do not provide services for chronic disease. Medical services for chronic conditions are available at designated hospitals. The fees incurred by treatment at designated hospitals or any other hospitals as well as any subsequent treatment are borne by delegates themselves.

但是,要注意,大型国际会议的会场和指定酒店的诊所通常不提供慢性病的医疗服务,只有指定医院提供慢性病的医疗服务。在指定医院或任何其他医院治疗所产生的费用及任何后续治疗费用须由与会代表自行承担。

To draw a conclusion, the preparatory work of LICs should be carried out with interactive divisions including conference programs, conference accommodation and venues, accreditation, contacts, international travel and domestic transport, media, security and health care, etc. During the preparation, a comprehensive and integrated set of guarantee plan including food and health care, security, transportation security, financial and logistical support should be constructed; a batch of well-qualified people with a deep understanding of politics, economy and English, including volunteers, are required to be recruited to form a relatively stable team in the taskforce; more importantly, the conference secretariat at all levels and each function group should jointly ensure that comprehensive cooperation is conducted and proper attention is paid to the fulfillment of all tasks.

总体来说,大型国际会议的筹备工作要通过会议日程、会议住宿与会场、注册工作、联络人员、国际旅程与国内交通、媒体、安保与医疗等工作分块联动展开。筹备期间需要构建一套包括餐饮和医疗保障、安全保障、交通保障、财务后勤保障等全方位、立体式的保障方案;需要选调、招募一批讲政治、懂经济、英文好的人员,包括志愿服务人员,形成相对稳定的办会队伍;更需要重点确保与大会秘书处各层级、各功能组进行全面对接,抓好工作落实。

2.2.2 Words, Phrases and Sentences 词汇、短语和例句

entourage 随行人员

careful deployment and repeated practice 精心部署和多次演练

conference program 会议日程

conference agenda 会议议程

the 2016 G20 Chinese Presidency Taskforce 2016 年 G20 中国筹备办

protocol channel 礼宾司渠道

shuttle bus 班车

designated 指定的

session venue 分会场

booth 同传箱

Delegation Contact Officer (DCO) 联络官

Delegation Accreditation Officer (DAO) 注册官

Liaison Officer (LO) 联络员

accreditation pass/badge 注册通行卡/代表证

non-transferable 不可互相转让的

logistics 后勤

Agreements on Mutual Visa Exemption 签证互免协议

customs declaration 海关报关

customs clearance 海关清关

carry-on baggage restriction 随身行李的限制

live stand-up position 现场直播区

briefing room 简报室

off-schedule activity 计划外活动安排

(1) Given that many readers are confused about the two concepts, conference programs and conference agenda, here it is made clear that conference programs include the conference agenda (i. e., the overall arrangements for the activity order related to the meeting topics) and other rituals or supportive activities during the conference.

鉴于许多读者都会混淆会议日程和会议议程两个概念,这里明确指出会议日程包括会议议程(即整个会议议题性活动顺序的总体安排)和会议期间的仪式性、辅助性的活动。

(2)…, during the Summit, foreign delegations were kindly requested to bring their own simultaneous interpreters as the host country only provided simultaneous interpretation between Chinese and English.

……在杭州峰会期间,欢迎外方代表团携带自己的同声传译员,主办国家只提供中英文之间的同声传译服务。

(3) From the perspective of LICs' accreditation, the accreditation aims to ensure every delegate's identity verification to participate in meetings and activities as well as their secure entry into the security venue/area.

从大型国际会议注册的角度来讲,注册是为了确保参加会议和活动的所有代表身份验证通过并能安全地进入安保会场/区域。

(4) It was important that delegates register for accreditation via the online accreditation portal as early as possible and then apply for their visas if necessary.

因此,对于代表们来说,尽早在网上注册平台完成注册,以便申请签证,显得至关重要。

(5) Except these listed countries, generally speaking, all other delegates from the LICs' member countries, guest counties or international organizations need valid visas or permits to enter China.

除了这些国家之外,通常,大型国际会议的成员、嘉宾或国际组织的所有代表都需要有效的签证或许可证方可进入中国境内。

(6) Given that airlines strictly enforce baggage size and weight limitations, delegates are requested to familiarize themselves with their airline luggage weight and carry-on baggage restrictions prior to traveling in order to avoid extra fees or complications.

鉴于航空公司严格执行行李尺寸和重量限制,请与会代表在旅行前熟悉自己的航空行李重量及航空公司对随身行李的限制,以避免产生额外费用或其他不必要的麻烦。

(7) To draw a conclusion, the preparatory work of LICs should be carried out with interactive divisions including conference programs, conference accommodation and venues, accreditation, contacts, international travel and domestic transport, media, security and health care, etc.

总体来说,大型国际会议的筹备工作要通过会议日程、会议住宿与会场、注册工作、联络人员、国际旅程与国内交通、媒体、安保与医疗等工作分块联动展开。

2. 2. 3 Situational Practice 情景演练

Case 1

This year it is the Chinese presidency for a LIC on Sustainable Development. You are a member of the conference taskforce. Now you are discussing the preparation work with your partner. You are welcome to refer to the dialogue below in which A represents you and B represents your partner.

今年轮到中国主办一个关于可持续发展的大型国际会议。你是会务筹备组的成员。现在你在和你的搭档讨论筹备工作。你可以参考下面的对话开展讨论,其中 A 代表你,B 代表你的搭档。

A:What do you think of the conference programs and agenda? Nowadays, as we know, the members of leading group are working on it almost night and day.

B:Yeah, sure. Because it's quite crucial and we really wanna seize the opportunity when it's our turn. I think the general schedule is already completed so we can elaborate on details. More specifically, put each procedure into its appropriate time unit.

A:I see. In addition, we are not only planning plenaries, bilateral and multilateral meetings, but also designing and selecting other ritual and supplementary activities such as dining or any gala. By the way, I've studied some materials on last year's conference in Japan, which is really helpful.

B:Really? What kind of materials?

A:It's the delegate handbook and executive curriculum of last year's conference. There is a huge amount of information we need. Though it took me lots of time, it's really worth it. Our colleagues have already translated it into Chinese as well.

B: That's brilliant. I should copy from your guys and look through them as well.

A: Sure. How has the online registration been going recently?

B: So far, everything has been going smoothly, however, the number of registered delegates is increasing not as fast as we expected.

A: Oh, in this case, we need to urge them a little bit.

B: True. We've been sending them e-mails usually. Some of them are lagging behind because they got problems with the online registration, so our colleagues are helping them out through e-mail communication.

A: Good job! I think it will work out finally.

A: 这几天领导小组都在夜以继日地研究会议日程和议程,你怎么看啊?

B: 是啊,当然啦。会议很重要,我们又真的很想抓住这次主办的机会。我觉得大概的议程已经完成了吧,现在我们就是要细化。就是说,要把每个环节安排到每个单位时间中去。

A: 我明白。而且,我们不仅要安排全体会议、双边和多边会议,还要设计和挑选其他的仪式性或者辅助性的活动,比如晚宴或者晚会什么的。对了,我最近仔细研究了去年日本主办时候的资料,还蛮有用的。

B: 真的吗? 哪方面的资料?

A: 就是去年的代表手册和行政须知,有很多我们需要的信息。我花了好长时间去看,不过很值得。我们的同事也已经把它们翻译成中文了。

B: 那太好了。我也要从你们那儿拷贝一份,仔细看看。

A: 可以啊。对了,最近代表的网上注册情况怎么样了?

B: 到目前来说,挺平稳的,但是代表注册的数量增长得没有我们之前预计的那么快。

A: 哦,那这样的话,我们要催着一点了。

B: 是啊。我们通常发电子邮件过去催。有些注册拖延是因为他们在线上注册遇到了问题,我们同事正在通过邮件交流帮他们解决这些问题。

A: 那太好了! 我觉得这个一定会起作用的。

Case 2

You are assigned as the Liaison Officer (LO) for Turkish delegation in a LIC on Environment Protection. In a few days, the delegation will arrive at Hangzhou Xiaoshan International Airport. What should you figure out before they arrive?

现有一场环保主题的大型国际会议,你被任命为负责土耳其代表团的联络员。几天后,土耳其代表团马上要到达杭州萧山国际机场了。在他们到达之前,你还要注意哪些问题?

Suggested plan (Please feel free to complement where there is an ellipsis mark):

参考计划(请在标有省略号的地方自由补充您的想法):

✓Be clear about the list of their delegation (including the size of the delegation, group leaders and even everyone's basic information)...

✓Figure out whether they have registered successfully online and their hotels have been booked...

✓Confirm with them the important schedules and never forget to ask them about any special requirement since it's easier to prepare for it in advance...

✓Review again the rituals and taboos of Turkish people...

✓清楚代表团名单(包括代表团规模、团队领导,甚至团里每个代表的基本信息)……

✓明确他们是否已经成功注册,他们的酒店是否预订好了……

✓和他们核对一些重要的议程。不要忘记提前询问他们有无特殊需求,以便尽早准备起来……

✓再次复习一下土耳其人的礼仪和禁忌……

2.2.4 Staff Interview 工作人员访谈

Based on the theme of this section, semi-structured interviews on the preparatory work of LICs have been conducted with the department staff under the taskforce's guidance. In the following third and fourth sections of Chapter 2, semi-structured interviews have also been carried out towards the summit volunteers and hotel staff according to the section content. Only through their hard work day and night and practical exploration can the prelude of the summit open and fall magnificently and can the world's attention stay in Hangzhou.

结合本节主题,我们围绕大型国际会议的筹备工作,对峰会筹备办指导下的部门工作人员开展了半结构式访谈。在 2.3,2.4 中,我们还将应章节内容的需求,对峰会志愿者和酒店工作人员进行半结构式访谈。在他们日日夜夜的努力工作下,在他们实践探索的前行中,峰会的序幕才得以华丽地开启而又落下,世界的目光才得以聚焦并且驻留杭州。

Semi-structured Interviews refer to informal interviews carried out according to a rough-and-ready interview outline. The method only has rough basic requirements towards the interviewees' conditions and the questions proposed so that the interviewers are allowed to flexibly make necessary adjustments according to the actual course of the interview. There are no specific requirements regarding the types of questions asked, answer format from interviewees, method for record-keeping, and the timing and location where the interview is conducted. In this way, the interviewer can deal with all situations in a flexible manner. Considering the privacy of all the interviewees, in this section, the following 3 interviewees are referred to as A, B and C.

半结构式访谈指按照一个粗线条式的访谈提纲进行的非正式的访谈。该方法对访谈对象的条件、所要询问的问题等只有一个粗略的基本要求,访谈者可以根据访谈时的实际情况灵活地做出必要的调整。至于提问的方式、访谈对象回答的方式、访谈记录的方式和访谈的时间、地点等没有具体的要求,由访谈者根据情况灵活处理。鉴于访谈对象的个人隐私保护,本小节中,用 A、B、C 来指称三位受访者。

2.2.4.1 Semi-structured Interview with A 对 A 的半结构式访谈

Q1: Hello! This interview is mainly about the preparation of LICs. Then, as a staff member of the G20, in your opinion, what are the differences between preparing for LICs such as the G20 and for other conferences in terms of difficulty degree, intensity and procedures?

提问 1:您好! 本次访谈主要是针对大型国际会议的筹备工作。那么您作为 G20 这样的大型国际会议的工作人员,在您亲身经历的筹备过程中,觉得在难度、强度和步骤上和准备其他会议有什么区别?

A: As we all know, the G20 Hangzhou Summit is seen as a political task, which is different from other international conferences. The official statement is that the G20 Summit is not only the most important domestic diplomatic activity of our country this year, but also an important vehicle for multilateral diplomacy. It is the mission and responsibility for each staff member of the G20 to make the Summit successful and historic, show the world the achievements China has made since the reform and opening-up policy, tell the world the story of China, and let Hangzhou impress the world.

A: 大家都知道,其实杭州承办 G20 本身也是一项政治任务,那么 G20 就有别于一般的国际会议。官方的说法是,G20 峰会是我国今年最重要的主场外交,也是今年中国多边外交的重要活动。办成一届精彩成功、载入史册的峰会,充分呈现中国改革开放以来的伟大成果,向全世界讲好中国故事,留下杭州印象,是每一名峰会筹备人员必须承担的历史使命和责任。

Q2: As a member of the conference staff, what do you think are the greatest challenges for Hangzhou to host the G20? Do you have any working experience to share with us?

提问 2: 作为会务工作人员,您觉得杭州承办峰会过程中最大的挑战是什么,或者您工作经验上有什么可以和我们分享的?

A: I think there are a lot of difficulties. Mentioning only some major ones among them, in my opinion, the largest difficulty is the lack of experience. Although Hangzhou has a good basis for hosting conferences, it lacks the experience of holding similar large-scale international conferences. A lot of work needs to be done from scratch. Secondly, it is the division of responsibilities. Unlike the province-level municipalities like Beijing and Shanghai, Hangzhou has to face the problem of the distribution of responsibilities, personnel and properties between the government of Hangzhou and Zhejiang Province, which is a great challenge. The third difficulty is regarding security. Security tasks embody a series of service guarantees in the main venue, B20, the fourth Sherpa Meeting, welcome dinner, the BRICS meeting, bilateral meetings and finance deputies' meetings.

A: 个人感觉承办的难点还是挺多的,如果要说几个首要的,我可以稍微提几个,比如说第一是缺少经验。杭州虽然有良好的办会基础,但是缺少承办类似大型国际会议的经验,很多工作都是从零开始。二是职责划分问题。筹备过程中,和北京、上海有所不同,杭州客观上存在浙江省、杭州市两级在人事财权上的划分界定问题,因此面临着一些挑战。三是保障任务繁重的问题,涉及主会场、B20、第四次协调人会议、欢迎晚宴、金砖会晤、双边会见、财政副手会议等一系列服务保障。

Q3: In terms of the main venue, is there any particular request for different stages of the preparation for LICs? Could you give us some suggestion according to your own experience?

提问 3: 那么大型国际会议筹备不同的阶段对主会场的会务工作有什么特别的要求呢? 您可以就您的经历或者了解的内容谈一谈吗?

A: Well, I will mention something about the conference work in the main venue according to my own experience. The work in the main venue focuses on the Leader's Summit. So, any mistakes are unacceptable. The heavy task is accompanied by high demands and pressure. The first stage is program preparation. New venues and changing requirements require the program preparation to be flexible yet still thorough. The second stage is the rehearsal for actual execution. In addition to the full-factor, full-view and full-flow rehearsal, some special drills should be organized to carry out verification, testing, continuous optimization and continuous improvement on the flow arrangement, material supply, facilities and equipment and emergency plans. The third stage is about emergency. Led by the Ministry of Foreign Affairs, the emergency support group for the main venue has been set up and responsible for the security and emergency response of all aspects of the meeting. Emergency personnel should be on duty at all time with quick response to ensure the success of the meeting.

A: 好的。那我就自己知道的具体说一下主会场的会务工作。主会场要承担领导人峰会会务,不能出半点差错,任务重,要求高,压力大。第一阶段是方案编写阶段。场馆新建和需求多变使得方案编写要做到千锤百炼。第二阶段是实战演练阶段。除了全要素、全实景、全流程演练外,还要组织一些专项演练,对方案执行流线安排、物资补给、设施设备、应急预案反复进行核验测试,不断优化,持续改进。第三阶段是会期应急阶段。由外交部牵头成立主会场应急保障小组,负责会议各个环节的安全防护和应急处理。会期应急人员实时待命,快速响应,以备一旦发生问题,能够最快衔接和处理,确保会议顺利进行。

Q4: What is your deepest impression of the whole preparation? Will it be beneficial to the following LICs which will be hosted in Zhejiang Province?

提问 4: 那么整个筹备过程中,从您的工作视角来看,让您感受最深的是什么? 可以为将来我们浙江省举办大型国际会议提供借鉴吗?

A: My experience is as follows. Firstly, Leaders at all levels have attached great importance and given proper guidance to the G20. Both in the preparatory stage of the meeting and during the formal meeting, the leaders of the central, provincial and municipal levels have personally conducted on-the-spot guidance, coordinated work and timely disposal of various emergencies to ensure the smooth progress of the meeting.

A：我的体会主要有：一是各级领导对 G20 峰会的高度重视和有力指挥。无论是会议筹备阶段还是正式会议期间,中央和浙江省各级领导都亲临现场指挥,统筹协调各项工作,及时处置各类紧急事件,确保了会议如期顺利进行。

Secondly, repeated exercises for a better summit. After each round of rehearsal, the organizing committee has convened a meeting to sort out and eradicated the problems found during the exercise, and constantly improved the meeting process.

二是为追求更好的会议效果反复演练。每次演练完毕,组委会都会及时召开会议梳理演练过程中发现的问题。针对发现的问题进行优化,不断完善会议流程。

Thirdly, the staff committed themselves into the preparatory work for the Summit. The taskforce has aimed closely at the goal of making the conference a complete success. All staff have done their best to achieve this goal, and earnestly fulfill the commitment of loyalty, probity and responsibility.

三是工作人员全身心投入到峰会筹备工作中。会务组紧紧围绕会议圆满成功这一目标,所有工作人员尽职尽责,切实履行了忠诚、正直、尽责的承诺。

Fourthly, it is the cooperation of different departments. Venue departments, exhibition companies, transport sectors, security agencies, health agencies and other departments all worked together to ensure the complete success of the G20 Hangzhou Summit which leaves Hangzhou and Zhejiang two valuable treasures. One is the experience of hosting large-scale international conferences; the other is the training for a more responsible and outstanding governor team.

四是各部门团结协作。场馆部、会展公司、交通部门、安保机构、卫计部门等各方面通力合作,助力 G20 杭州峰会圆满成功。通过这次峰会筹办,杭州乃至浙江获得了两笔宝贵财富,一是获得了主办大型国际会议的经验,二是锻炼出一支具有责任感、素质过硬的干部队伍。

2.2.4.2 Semi-structured interview with B 对 B 的半结构式访谈

Q1: Hello! This interview is mainly about the preparation of LICs. Then, as a staff member of the G20, in your opinion, what are the differences between preparing for LICs such as the G20 and for other conferences in terms of difficulty degree, intensity and procedures?

提问 1：您好！本次访谈主要是针对大型国际会议的筹备工作。那么您作为 G20 这样的大型国际会议的工作人员，在您亲身经历的筹备过程中，觉得在难度、强度和步骤上和准备其他会议有什么区别？

B：Of course. Unlike other meetings, the online platform of large-scale international conferences should be verified rigorously in view of the importance and rigor of content. For example, we can see directly from the data statistics that the official website of the Summit and related links have a high page view with global attention. As a meeting for the world's 20 most important countries, economies, and global organizations, the quality of visits and log-in determines the reputation and influence of the site.

B：这个当然是不大一样的。不同于其他会议，大型国际会议在网上平台的安全规划中，鉴于内容的重要性和严谨性，网站内容必须经过严格的层层审核。比如我们可以从数据统计上直观地看出，因全球关注，峰会官网和相关链接的访问频率极高。作为一个有全球 20 个重要国家和经济体，以及多个重量级世界组织参加的大会，网站访问和登录的质量决定了网站的名誉度和影响力。

Q2：As a staff member of the Summit Network Security, what impact do you think the Summit will have on the security of websites and related information systems?

提问 2：作为峰会网络保障的工作人员，您觉得峰会在全球的影响力会对网站和相关信息系统的安全带来什么影响？

B：Due to the huge influence of the G20 Summit, different types of hacking attempts accompanied by a high page view threatened information safety of the Summit. The threat has involved two aspects. Firstly, the 24-hour continous attacks were from different parts of the world. Secondly, there were various techniques of attacks which put a test on the technical skills of our technicians. Therefore, the working demands were so high that our workers had to work round-the-clock.

B：由于峰会的影响巨大，来自全球的访问量也非常大，来自全球不同方式的网络攻击使信息安全面临巨大挑战。这个挑战体现在两个方面，一是攻击来自全球不同区域，24 小时不间断；二是全球的攻击手法千变万化，极其考验我们技术员的实力。所以我们的工作人员任务繁重，工作夜以继日。

Q3：It is really hard work to serve such an important summit. Well, the next question is about the respective requirements of information security for different preparation stages of LICs. What is the importance of information security in the last stage of the conference?

提问 3: 是啊,保障如此重要的峰会,你们真是辛苦了。好的,那么我们再来谈一谈您觉得大型国际会议筹备在不同的阶段对网络信息安全有什么特别的要求,特别是在筹备期的最后冲刺阶段?

B: At different stages, the focus and intensity of work are different. For a LIC with a number of participating countries and international organizations, the network traffic may not climb to the maximum level during the daytime, because we serve the global users. Due to time gaps, the evening is likely to become the peak of the visit. This requires the organizing committee to take rotations to ensure that the network is in operation and maintenance from day to night. Almost everyone would feel nervous about a month before the Leaders' Summit.

B: 在不同阶段,工作的重心和强度是不同的。对于一个参与国家和世界组织众多的大型国际会议而言,网络访问量并不是白天最高,这是因为我们服务的是全球网友,由于时差关系,晚上很有可能成为访问高峰期。这就要求组委会实行轮岗制来保证网络 24 小时都有人在运行维护。在领导人峰会召开前一个月,几乎所有人都会感到紧张。

Q4: What is your deepest impression of the whole preparation? Is it beneficial to the following LICs which will be hosted in Zhejiang Province?

提问 4: 那么整个筹备过程中,从您的工作视角来看,您最深的感受是什么?可以为下次我们浙江省举办大型国际活动提供什么借鉴?

B: Large international conferences have higher requirements on the network platform in terms of real-time stability and reliability. The various stages of the meeting all have a common requirement of the network, namely the network information security. Network information security mainly refers to the security which ensures that the data cannot be tampered with or leaked, and webpages cannot be tampered with. In terms of technique, we were faced with network attacks from all over the world, in the last line of defense human intelligence is necessary to analyze, to determine, and to decide countermeasures.

B: 大型国际会议对网络平台的实时性、稳定性、可靠性方面有更高的要求。

会议的各个阶段对互联网都有一个共同的要求,就是网络信息安全。网络信息安全主要就是指数据不能被篡改、不能被泄露,网页不能被篡改。从技术方面来讲,我们面对的是来自全世界的网络攻击,在最后的一道网络防线上还是需要用人的智慧去分析,去判断,去决定对策。

2.2.4.3 Semi-structured interview with C 对 C 的半结构式访谈

Q1: Hello! This interview is mainly about the preparation of LICs. Then, as a staff member of the G20, in your opinion, what are the differences between preparing for LICs such as the G20 and for other conferences in terms of the degree of difficulty, intensity and procedures?

提问 1: 您好! 本次访谈主要是针对大型国际会议的筹备工作。那么您作为 G20 这样的大型国际会议的工作人员,在您亲身经历的筹备过程中,觉得在难度、强度和步骤上和准备其他会议有什么区别?

C: As a front-line worker, I've participated in planning the district-level working conference before. During this time, it's a huge honor for me to participate in an international event such as the G20 and of course I also benefited a lot from my participation. In general, no matter in terms of the degree of difficulty, time span, work intensity or preparation steps, LICs such as the G20 exceed much more than city-level meetings.

C: 作为一名基层工作人员,我曾经参与策划过区级层面的工作会议,这次有幸能够参与 G20 这种国际盛会,我感到无比荣幸,当然也获益匪浅。总的来说,像 G20 这样的大型国际会议无论是难度、时间跨度、工作强度,还是准备步骤都比市区级别的会议要高出不只一个等级。

In particular, as for the conference size, an international summit involves many countries and international organizations, which requires the conference organizers to be equipped with multi-lingual talents. At the same time, many countries and international organizations may be located in different time zones, which requires conference organizers to provide prolonged service to cover all these time zones to meet the delegates' needs from different time zones. In addition, LICs put forward higher requirements for timeliness, accuracy and confidentiality, which requires the staff to have higher comprehensive quality and ability to work under pressure. Finally, LICs have quite a lot preparation steps, for example, before the Leaders' Summit, there had been already more than 30 related meetings held and lots of on-spot practice for accreditation. In a word, what mentioned above all suggests the particularity of LICs.

具体来说，国际峰会在规模上涉及的国家或者国际组织众多，这就给会议主办方提出了需要多语人才的要求。同时，这些国家和国际组织可能分属不同时区，这就要求会议主办方需要提供更长时间跨度的服务，以便适应不同时区参会代表的要求。而且，大型国际会议无论是对工作的时效性、准确性还是对保密性都提出了非常高的要求，这就要求工作人员具备更高的综合素质和更强的抗压能力。最后，国际会议的会议准备步骤也非常多，例如本次峰会之前的系列会议就开了 30 余场，针对峰会的注册演练也进行了多次，这都说明了大型国际会议的特殊性。

Q2: From the accreditation perspective of LICs, as one of the staff, what kind of difficulties did Hangzhou face or what kind of similar working experience can you share with us?

提问 2:从大型国际会议的注册工作来讲，作为工作人员，你觉得杭州承办峰会遇到了什么问题/困难，或者您工作经验上有什么可以和我们分享的？

C: Firstly, the overall internationalization of Hangzhou relatively needs to be improved, such as the English popularity. Regarding the English level of government websites or civil servants, it is still at a low starting point, compared with the Shanghai government website since there are English version websites even for the street-level government in Shanghai. If we want more foreigners to know and fall in love with Hangzhou, we should at the same time strengthen the English education of civil servants and add websites for foreign interaction. It will enable foreigners to directly ask questions through the website and get answers in their languages.

C: 首先是杭州整体的国际化程度相对来说还有待提高，比如说英语普及度还需提高。较之上海的政务网站，目前杭州无论是政府网站还是公务人员的英语水平都处于一个起点较低的位置，上海连街道级官网都有了英文版本。杭州若想让更多外国人认识杭州，喜爱杭州，应同时加强对公务人员的英语教育，并增加一个对外的互动网站，让外国人可以直接在网站上提问并获得对应语言的回答。

LICs call for the common cooperation among many functional departments. Take the Summit as an example, based on the former municipal government structure, Hangzhou temporarily built up a new organizational structure—"One Office with Nine Departments" featuring the labor division in cooperation and achieved success in the end. But if Hangzhou wants to position itself as an international conference city or a number of international conferences pick up Hangzhou as the destination, a standing department specific for meeting preparation needs to be set up instead of a temporary taskforce like G20's, with more professionals undertaking the organizing and other aspects of the meeting and accumulating experience. A professional taskforce should be trained to undertake future international conferences for Hangzhou.

大型国际会议需要众多职能部门的通力合作。就此次峰会来说,杭州市临时以市机关部门为骨架组建"一办九部",分工合作筹备峰会,取得了成功。但若今后杭州将自身定位为一个国际会议城市,或是每年都有一定数量的国际会议落户杭州的话,就需要成立一个专门的会议筹备部门而不是峰会筹委会这样的临时组织,更加专业地承接会议组织、召开等各方面的工作,并且不断积累经验,为杭州培养一支职业的国际会议承办队伍。

Q3: Well, the next question is about the respective requirements for accreditation work in different preparation stages of LICs. Can you talk a bit about it in terms of your work?

提问 3:那么大型国际会议筹备不同的阶段对注册方面的工作有什么特别的要求呢?您可以就您经历的或了解的谈一谈吗?

C: The preparation of LICs often lasts a long time. For example, the accreditation work of the Summit appeared to last just more than a month from late July to early September, but actually from the 1st Sherpa Meeting a year ago, the accreditation work had already been under rehearsal, accumulation and adjustment. The 38 series meetings served by the Accreditation Centre throughout the whole preparatory year actually had paved the way for the final summit meeting. So I think such a long preparation process is very rare in our experiences.

C: 大型会议的准备阶段往往时间很长,像这次峰会的注册工作虽然看似是从 7 月底到 9 月初这一个多月,但是其实在一年前的第一次协调人峰会开始,就已经在为峰会注册工作进行预演、积累和调整了。全年注册中心服务的 38 场系列会议其实都是在为最后的峰会做铺垫。因此这么长的一个准备过程我觉得是非常罕见的。

Looking back on it now, during the on-spot registration of the Summit, if the badge rules were made too complicated or difficult for the delegates to understand, it would create more inconvenience, regardless of participant delegations or the Accreditation Centre. Of course the security at the conference is important, but if the excessive emphasis on security or the security convenience brought complex registration and cumbersome effect to the meeting itself, I personally think it would focus too much on trifles and neglect essentials. Because the security service works for the conference, we should give priority to convenient registration. Blind pursuit of security, on the contrary, would lead foreign delegates to spend more time and energy to get their badges, thus influencing their attendance.

在峰会正式现场注册阶段,现在回过头来看,如果证件方案过于复杂或较难让代表理解,就会造成较多不便,不管对参会代表团还是对注册中心来说都是如此。会议的安保问题固然重要,但是如果因为过度强调安保或者为安保便利而使得会议注册复杂、烦琐到影响会议本身进行的话,我个人认为是舍本逐末。因为安保工作是为会议这个主题进行服务的,应该以会议注册便利为优先,一味追求安全反而会让外国代表花费更多的时间和精力拿到证件,影响参会。

Q4: So during the whole preparation process, from your perspective, what is your deepest impression? Can it provide any reference for the following large international activities held in Zhejiang?

提问 4:那么整个筹备过程中,从您的工作视角来看,您最深的感受是什么?可以为下次我们浙江省举办大型国际活动提供什么借鉴?

C: During the entire preparation process, the mutual understanding and cooperation by all the citizens of the preparation work for the G20 gave me the deepest impression. No matter they are uncles, aunts or children, local residents or outsiders, they were all willing to sacrifice in order to successfully hold the Summit. We saw in all walks of life, basic English were taught and learned to facilitate our foreign guests when necessary. Many buildings had been demolished and some residential facades had been restored, which though disturbed citizens' daily life, but what we found were only support and understanding. It was the efforts and sacrifice by every local and outsider in Hangzhou that promoted the smooth operation of this Summit. So I am full of confidence in Hangzhou and the whole Zhejiang Province to undertake large international activities in the future because we have such a lovely group of respectable people in Hangzhou and all of Zhejiang.

C: 整个筹备过程中,我印象最深的就是全市人民对于 G20 峰会所有筹备工作的理解和配合。无论男女老幼,无论是本地市民还是外来人员,都愿意为了峰会的顺利举办付出或者牺牲小我。我们看到各行各业都在努力学习基础英语,以便能够在必要的时候为外宾提供便利。许多建筑被拆除,小区外面被重新修缮,这些都对市民的日常生活产生了影响,但是我们看到的只有支持和理解。正是有了每一个杭州市民和外来人员的努力和付出,这场盛事才得以顺利举办。所以我对杭州乃至浙江今后承办大型国际活动充满了信心,因为我们拥有这样一批可爱可敬的杭州人、浙江人。

2.2.5 Extensive Links 拓展链接

In a LIC, as the first common language, English acts not only in the form of speaking but also of writing. In this section, we'll talk about how to carry out e-mail communication in English with foreign guests. Since e-mail is the main channel of communication for LICs, what are the elements that we should pay attention to?

在大型国际会议中,英语作为第一通用语言,除了以说的形式存在之外,还以写这一重要形式存在。本小节,我们就来谈谈如何与外宾进行英文邮件往来。邮件往来是大型国际会议中交流的主要方式,那么其中有哪些要素是我们要注意的呢?

Firstly, of course the principle of politeness is high-lighted. This principle not only means the prohibition of using inappropriate or insulting words, but also means the awareness to use polite words.

首先,要注意的是礼貌原则。礼貌原则并不是说只要没有不得体或侮辱性的言语就是礼貌,而是指要学会应用礼节性词语的意识。

For example, when you receive letters, you need to reply with appreciation or regards in the beginning, "Thank you for your letter" or "We acknowledge with many thanks in receipt of your letter." In addition, even in an emergency, try to avoid some hard imperative or mandatory words. For example, "You are cordially/kindly requested to send your itineraries in advance so that we can arrange the transport" sounds much better, instead of "We order/ask you to send your itineraries in advance so that we can arrange the transport." Besides, though you've answered many questions, keep patient and put forward friendly in the end of the letter to welcome their feedback if they have any other problem. It is advised to write like this, "If you have any other problems, please let us know" or "If you experience any difficulties performing this task, please feel free to contact us. "

比如收到对方的来信,在回信的时候,往往以感谢或问候开头,"感谢您的来信"或"收到您的来信,我们十分感激"。另外,即便十分紧急,也尽量避免用一些生硬的命令性或强制性词语。比如,与其用"我们命令/要求你提前发行程过来以便我们安排接送",不如用"我们真诚地/友善地提醒您提前发行程过来以便我们安排接送"。除此之外,即便你已经为对方解答了很多问题,也要保持一颗平常心而不要急躁,在邮件结尾可以友好地表示如若还有任何问题,欢迎对方来信咨询。建议可以这么写,"如果您还有其他任何问题,可以来信告知我们"或者"如果您在做这件事的时候遇到了困难,随时联系我们"。

Secondly, please pay attention to the principle of confidentiality. E-mails usually contain important information of an individual or a group, therefore, the principle of confidentiality not only refers to e-mail accounts and password management, but also proper letter writing which reassures each other's confidentiality. For example, while providing account and password to another party, it is suggested to make it clear that this is their proprietary account and password which won't be known by any third party. You can write as "The user-name and password provided are exclusive for you. "

其次,请注意保密原则。邮件往来中通常涉及个人或集团的重要信息,因此,保密原则不仅仅指管好邮箱账号密码,也可以体现在信件写作中,从而让对方安心、舒心。比如向对方提供某个平台账号密码的时候,可以说明这是对方专有的账号密码,不再有第三方知晓,"我们提供给你们专属的账号和密码"。

Thirdly, when it comes to a political international conference, being politically sensitive is necessary. The so-called "No issues in diplomacy are small", tells us that free writing in lack of political sensitivity either lightly breaks each other's taboo to damage self-image, or even leads to disputes in foreign affairs. For example, do not denigrate any political stance, or while urging others, make sure we have proof to remind others of the deadline. You can write like this, "As stated in the Administrative Circular, all delegates attending the meeting must be accredited before 24:00, May 6(GMT+8)" or "As stipulated in the schedule, please be advised that the portal will remain available until 24:00, May 6 (GMT+8). "

再次,若是政治性国际会议,要具备政治敏感性。所谓"外交无小事",缺乏政治敏感性的随意写作,轻则触犯到对方的禁忌,有损自我形象,重则会导致外事纠纷。比如不可诋毁任何政治立场;在催促对方、提醒对方截止日期的时候,要有据可依。可以这样表示:"按照行政须知上的规定,所有参会代表必须在北京时间 5 月 6 日 24 点前注册"或"按照议程上的说明,我们友情提醒一下,平台将于北京时间 5 月 6 日 24 点关闭"。

At last, the accuracy cannot be neglected. No matter how fancy the polite words are in a letter, if there are obvious or too many vocabulary and grammar mistakes, it will leave a bad impression on the receiver.

最后,准确性不能疏忽。一封信礼貌用语再花哨,但如果有明显或过多的词汇和语法错误,就会给对方留下不好的印象。

2.3 Volunteer Service for Conferences
会议志愿服务

2.3.1 Brief Introduction 简介

Heavy, demanding, difficult, and complicated are typical characteristics of conference tasks of LICs. Whether conference work is carried out in a good or bad way has an important and direct impact on the conference's quality. In order to ensure the success of the conference work and the success of the meeting, manpower is an essential precondition, as well as the cooperation of all the departments. To solve the problem of manpower, volunteers become an important part in taskforce work.

大型会议的会务工作任务重、要求高、难度大,极为繁杂。会务工作做得好坏,是影响会议质量和会议效果好坏的重要因素。为了确保会务工作的顺利和会议的成功,大量的人力投入及各方的配合都是必要前提。从解决人力问题的角度来讲,志愿者工作就成了筹备组工作中重要的一部分。

Volunteers, especially the teachers and students in the universities, who are equipped with professional knowledge and foreign language ability, have become an important part in every conference. From the preparation to the end of the meeting, volunteers may participate in any part. In a word, volunteers consitute an indispensible section for the preparation and processing of LICs.

志愿者,特别是各高校教师和学生志愿者,拥有较高的专业知识及语言等相关知识储备,在各类会议的会务工作中,志愿者已成为其中重要的一部分。从前期筹备到会议服务直至会议结束,任何一个环节都可能会有志愿者的参与。志愿者在大型国际会议的筹备和举办过程中也是不可缺少的一部分。

As a key part of meeting services, volunteers' tasks are not just to complete their job, but also to carry the responsibility of language communication and cultural exchange. Volunteer service for guests is also a channel to promote the nation and the state, as well as peace, friendship, and mutual aid.

志愿者作为会议服务中的重要环节,他们的任务不仅仅只是完成自己的岗位工作,还承载着语言沟通、文化交流的任务。志愿者为服务对象服务的过程也就是向对方宣传一个民族和国家,宣传和平、友谊、互助的过程。

Figure 2-8   Volunteer Mobilization Activities before G20 Summit
图 2-8   G20 杭州峰会志愿者动员活动

Compared with other types of volunteers, such as those serving with communities or games, volunteers of LICs need not only volunteer spirits and high-quality service skills, but also refined qualities: excellent language skills, good understanding of the corresponding conference knowledge, brilliant awareness of the host city and country's traditional history and culture, and good foreign-related etiquette. Volunteers work mainly covers airport reception, accreditation, media center, venues, hotels and road guidance, company, interpretation and so on. Taking the volunteers in the G20 Hangzhou Summit as an example, there are totally 3,760 volunteers recruited from 15 universities and colleges.

与社区服务志愿者或运动会志愿者等其他类型不同,大型国际会议志愿者除了要有志愿者精神和优质的志愿者服务技能技巧之外,还要具备优良的素质:拥有精湛的语言技能,了解相应会议知识,熟知举办城市及国家的历史文化,具有良好的涉外礼仪等。志愿者的工作主要有机场接待,注册制证,新闻宣传,会场、酒店、道路引导,陪同、翻译等。以 G20 峰会志愿者工作为例,会议期间共招募 3760 名志愿者,来自杭州 15 所高校。

Volunteers assigned to each department is responsible for a different mission but all are closely linked. For example, the G20 Accreditation Center is mainly in charge of the management of each delegation's e-mails, collection of accreditation information, badges collection, etc.

会务志愿者各自负责的工作任务不同,但相互之间紧密联系。例如,在 G20 杭州峰会举办期间,注册中心主要负责代表团注册邮件回复、与会代表信息收集整理、证件发放等工作。

For every conference volunteer, dealing with every important issue properly is vital. Volunteers also need to have a clear understanding of their work, and to make adequate mental preparation. Most of the volunteers may be engaged in some tedious work such as road guidance and hotel guidance. But from another perspective, it is the volunteer work as it instinctively is, ordinary but meaningful.

对于每一位会务志愿者来说,做好每一件小事都很重要。志愿者还需要对其工作性质有清醒的认识,并做好充分的心理准备。大多数志愿者可能从事的是一些例如道路引导、酒店引导等单调乏味的工作,但这就是志愿者的工作,平凡却有意义。

The volunteer project in Zhejiang Province began in 1993. Over the last 20 years, under attention and support of Zhejiang Provincial Party Committee, the Provincial Government and other party committees and governments at all levels, at the same time with the strong support and active participation from the society, volunteer service organizations have firmly been based on the overall work of the provincial party committee and the basic needs of people's livelihood. They have played an active role in poverty alleviation, large-scale activities, community services, environmental protection, disaster relief and many other areas.

浙江省的志愿者行动始于 1993 年,20 多年来,在浙江省委、省政府及各级党委政府的重视、关心和支持下,在社会各界的大力支持和积极参与下,全省各级志愿服务组织紧紧围绕省委、省政府工作大局和人民群众生产生活的基本需求,在扶贫帮困、大型活动、社区服务、环境保护、抢险救灾等众多领域发挥了积极的作用。

In terms of activities, the volunteer service in Zhejiang Province is divided into four major categories: assisting volunteer service projects, mainly for vulnerable groups and the masses; professional volunteer projects; public welfare volunteer service projects; and games and conference volunteer service projects.

在活动方面,浙江省的志愿服务主要分为四大类项目:援助性志愿服务项目,主要面向社会弱势群体和困难群众;专业性志愿者项目;公益性志愿服务项目;赛会志愿服务项目。

With the LICs such as the West Lake Expo, the China-LAC Business Summit and the G20 Summit held in Hangzhou, Hangzhou's ability of holding LICs is gradually being upgraded to conform to international standards.

随着西湖博览会、中国—拉美企业家高峰会、G20峰会等大型国际会议在杭州召开,杭州的办会水平正逐渐提升,与国际接轨。

2.3.2 Words, Phrases and Sentences 词汇、短语和例句

conference volunteer 会务志愿者
backbone volunteer 骨干志愿者
Badge-making Centre 制证中心
Accreditation Centre 注册中心
Media Centre 新闻中心
company/accompanying volunteer 陪同(志愿者)
badge collection 证件发放
public welfare volunteer service 公益性志愿服务
the West Lake Expo 西博会
the China-LAC Business Summit 中国—拉美企业家高峰会

(1)Whether conference work is carried out in a good or bad way has an important and direct impact on the conference's quality.

会务工作做得好坏,是影响会议质量和会议效果好坏的重要因素。

(2)Most of the volunteers may be engaged in some tedious work such as road guidance and hotel guidance. But from another perspective, it is the volunteer work as it instinctively is, ordinary but meaningful.

大多数志愿者可能从事的是一些例如道路引导、酒店引导等单调乏味的工作,但这就是志愿者的工作,平凡却有意义。

(3)With the LICs such as the West Lake Expo, the China-LAC Business Summit and the G20 Summit held in Hangzhou, Hangzhou's ability of holding LICs is gradually being upgraded to conform to international standards.

随着西湖博览会、中国—拉美企业家高峰会、G20 峰会等大型国际会议在杭州召开,杭州的办会水平正逐渐提升,与国际接轨。

2.3.3 Situational Practice 情景演练

In the cases below, DAO is the term for Delegation Accreditation Officer, V is short for volunteer, D is short for delegate while R is short for reporter.

在以下案例中,注册官的专用术语为 DAO,V 代表志愿者,D 代表参会代表,R 代表记者。

Case 1

There is a delegate from a foreign delegation coming to the Accreditation Centre for badge collection, but he/she is not sure about whether his/her online registration is successfully done.

国外代表团代表前来注册中心领取证件,但是他/她不确定自己是否已成功进行网上注册。

V:Good morning, welcome to the Accreditation Center. May I help you?

D:Morning, I'm going to collect my ID badges.

V:Have you done online registration before?

D:Sorry, I am not sure.

V:Which delegation are you in? Please give me your passport. I'll check it for you.

D:OK. Here you are.

V:Hello sir, you have registered online, so please go to the No. 1 Collection Desk to collect your badge.

D: Thank you so much. Can I collect ID badges for my colleagues?

V: I am so sorry. Only DAO can collect ID badges for other delegates.

D: But you know, our DAO is now on the flight so that I cannot get in touch with him. And he will arrive very late.

V: Sir, we sincerely apologize that you still can't collect others' badges. Your DAO can do it after arriving. Or your colleagues can come and collect themselves.

志愿者:上午好! 欢迎来到注册中心。有什么可以为您效劳的吗?

代表:早上好,我来这里领取证件。

志愿者:请问您之前进行过网上注册了吗?

代表:我不太清楚。

志愿者:请问您来自哪个代表团? 请出示一下您的护照,我们可以帮您查询一下。

代表:好的。

志愿者:您好,您已经在网上注册过,您可以直接领取证件。请前往1号台证件发放处。

代表:谢谢。请问我可以帮同事代领证件吗?

志愿者:不好意思,只有DAO可以代领证件。

代表:我们代表团的DAO现在在飞机上,要很迟才能抵达,实在不方便来领取证件。

志愿者:真的抱歉,DAO抵达后可以来替您的同事领取,或者请您的同事自己过来领取。

Conclusion: During the service, volunteers may encounter that some guests put forward requirements which are beyond the rules. Most of volunteers will try their best to meet the guests' needs or even cater for them. Actually, there are certain rules of international conferences that everyone shall obey. Therefore, our volunteers should be polite and neither too humble nor too pushy.

总结:志愿者在服务中,可能会遇到外宾提出不符合规定的要求,大部分志愿者会尽全力满足外宾的要求,有时甚至会过度迎合别人。然而,任何会议或者活动都有相应的规则,每一个人都应该遵守。因此,志愿者在做到有礼有节的同时,还要不卑不亢。

Case 2

Some reporters want to do an interview with volunteers.

在志愿者值班期间遇到记者采访。

R：May I do an interview with you?

V：I'm so sorry that I am on duty so it is not suitable for me to do the interview.

（The reporter still insists on doing the interview.）

V：Sorry. According to the regulations, we cannot accept the interview.

R：We only need to ask several simple questions.

V：If you must do the interview, please contact the volunteer center or our head. Thank you for your cooperation.

记者：请问可以采访你一下吗？

志愿者：不好意思，我正在工作，不能接受采访。

（记者仍想继续采访）

志愿者：不好意思，按照规定我们不能接受采访。

记者：我们只需要简单问几个问题就好了。

志愿者：不好意思，如果您需要采访的话，您可以先和志愿者中心联系或者和我们的负责人联系。谢谢您的配合。

Conclusion：Volunteers must obey the arrangements of conference taskforce and cannot accept interviews freely. If necessary, permission of a superior is needed.

总结：作为一名志愿者，要服从会务安排，不能随意接受记者采访。如必须接受采访，需要得到上级许可。

Case 3

The delegate consults the volunteer for rental vehicles.

代表询问志愿者租车问题。

D：Hello, I'd like to know if you will provide rental vehicles.

V：Yes. We have rental vehicles services, but all the vehicles must be accredited to enter the Hangzhou International Expo Center. Accreditation requests will be allowed for sedan cars, minivans and vans only. Drivers of these vehicles should be accredited as well.

D: Then how can I be accredited for the cars and drivers?

V: Vehicle accreditation can be made through your designated Liaison Officer. After the accreditation, Vehicle Access Passes will be issued via your designated Liaison Officers. We recommend you rent chauffeured vehicles from the designated Zhejiang Zetastone Financial Leasing Co., Ltd. Please contact the manager for inquiries related to the available types of vehicles, pricing, and reservation.

代表: 你好,请问你们这边可以租车吗?

志愿者: 可以的,但是租用车辆只有经过注册方可进入杭州国际博览中心。只有轿车、小型货车和厢式货车才允许注册。车辆司机也须经过注册。

代表: 那我要怎么给车辆和司机进行注册?

志愿者: 租用车辆可通过中方联络官注册。注册后,车辆通行证会通过中方联络官发放。我们建议您从指定租车公司浙江中大元通融资租赁有限公司租车,关于车型、报价、预订可以联系他们的负责人。

2.3.4 Volunteers Interview 志愿者访谈

In this book, we have interviewed three volunteers from G20 Accreditation Center and two from the third World Internet Conference (Wuzhen Summit). Five students are labelled here as S1 to S5.

本书中,我们采访了三位 G20 注册中心的志愿者和两位第三届世界互联网大会乌镇峰会的志愿者。五位学生分别用 S1 到 S5 表示。

In the G20 Accreditation Center, there is a special volunteer team made up of 13 postgraduate students recruited from School of Foreign Languages, Zhejiang Gongshang University. These 13 backbone volunteers belong to the first batch of G20 volunteers. From November 2015 onwards, they began to have a series of training and then much actual practice. Before the G20 Hangzhou Summit, they have already served in Sanya G20 Finance and Central Bank Deputy Meeting (the first G20 meeting in China), the first G20 Sherpa Meeting in Beijing, the second G20 Sherpa Meeting in Guangzhou, the third G20 Sherpa Meeting in Xiamen, G20 Meeting of Agricultural Ministers in Xi'an.

G20 注册中心的骨干志愿者是全国最早的一批 G20 志愿者,由浙江工商大学外国语学院 13 位研究生组成。从 2015 年 11 月起,他们便参加了一系列培训和实战,先后服务于三亚 G20 财政和央行副手会(中国 G20 会议的首场会议)、北京 G20 第一次协调人会议、广州 G20 第二次协调人会、厦门 G20 第三次协调人会议、西安 G20 农业部部长会议。

Another three students interviewed volunteered as the one-to-one accompanying volunteers for VIP delegates in the third World Internet Conference. It posed high requirements for their personal characters, language skills and international views. Through this interview, we hope to take a glimpse of their daily accompanying work.

另外三位受访者是第三届世界互联网大会的志愿者,负责重要嘉宾的一对一陪同,对志愿者的品格素质、语言技能和国际视野三方面的要求都较高。通过此次访谈,我们也可以来看看他们的陪同日常。

S1 to S3 are the G20 Summit volunteers.

学生 S1 到 S3 是 G20 峰会的志愿者。

2.3.4.1 Semi-structured interview with S1 对 S1 的半结构式访谈

Q1: Have you participated in other volunteer work before?

提问 1:之前有参加过志愿者活动吗?

S1: Well, actually I think my volunteer service experiences are quite rich. From junior high school to university, I have always been the president of students' union, and participated in various types of volunteer activities. I led the summer school team to voluntarily teach in the countryside and raised education funds to carry out various activities for the mountain children. I actively took part in and organized the volunteer work of China International Cartoon & Animation Festival. I also participated in the National Intelligent Car Race Finals as the site host. Moreover, I took the initiative to participate in various types of community and school volunteer activities. In a word, volunteer work is addictive for me.

S1: 嗯,志愿服务经历还比较丰富。从初中到大学,我一直担任学生会主席,也是各类志愿活动的参与者和负责人。我曾带领校暑期志愿团队下乡支教,募集教育基金,开展各项活动,为山区的孩子带去欢乐和希望;积极参与和组织了中国国际动漫节的志愿活动;还参加过全国智能汽车竞赛总决赛的志愿工作,担任现场主持的工作;同时还积极参与各类社区志愿活动和校志愿活动。志愿工作会上瘾。

Q2：So how did you know and become a G20 volunteer?

提问 2：你是怎么成为 G20 志愿者的?

S1：Around October, 2015, I participated in the volunteer interview organized by our school, and after various tests and interview selection, I finally became one of the G20 backbone volunteers. Then we also took a series of training to enhance the operational capacity to be a qualified G20 volunteer.

S1：2015 年 10 月,我参加了学院组织的志愿者面试,经过层层考察和面试选拔,成为 G20 志愿者骨干之一。之后还通过一系列培训,增强业务能力,成为一名合格的 G20 志愿者。

Q3：How do you feel about this volunteer experience?

提问 3：这次志愿者经历有什么感受?

S1：Actually volunteers of the G20 Hangzhou Summit were busy. On weekends, I must learn relevant knowledge and practice our skills while others were relaxing. On holidays, I need to be on duty while other students went back home. In the preparatory days of the Summit, I had been to Guangzhou with seven other backbone volunteers and participated in the accreditation of the second G20 Sherpa meeting. It was through the actual experience that I were aware of the complexity and importance of the G20 onsite registration work. Busy but significant.

S1：峰会志愿者工作很繁忙。周末,别人在休息时,我和其他骨干志愿者们在学习业务知识,练习业务技能;寒暑假,其他学生都回家时,我们依然要值班,坚守岗位。峰会前期,我和其他七名骨干一起去过广州,参与第二次协调人会议的注册工作。通过实战,我第一次感受到了 G20 注册现场工作的复杂性和重要性。虽然忙碌,但是意义重大。

Q4：What capacity and quality do you think are necessary for a good conference volunteer or just for an accreditation center volunteer?

提问 4：你认为一个优秀的会务志愿者,或者注册中心志愿者,需要哪些能力和品质?

S1：As far as I am concerned, a good conference volunteer needs a strong operational capacity. We, 13 backbone volunteers, are assigned as team leaders for different functional areas. Our job was not only to lead the team members to learn business knowledge, to repeat scene exercises, to build and manage the team, but also to participate in the preparation of volunteer workbooks, team work program development, e-mail response to countries and organizations and so on. However, the diverse distribution of each delegation around the world, the complex e-mail content and frequent e-mail exchanges, all put a great test for language skills and comprehensive qualities on us.

S1: 据我所知,一名优秀的会务志愿者需要很强的业务能力。我们 13 名骨干组成的各功能区组长团队,不仅要带领组员学习业务知识,反复情景演练,进行团队建设,还要参与志愿者工作手册编写、小组工作方案制定、各参会国家和组织的邮件回复、注册预约工作等。其中,由于所负责代表团分布世界各地,邮件内容复杂,往来频繁,这项工作极大地考验了我们的语言水平和综合素质。

Q5: What impressed you most during the service?

提问 5: 服务期间有哪些令你印象深刻的事?

S1: The conference volunteer team is very united and warm. Everyone, from the directors, the school leaders, to staff and teachers, is quite concerned about the volunteers. The accreditation center looks like a big warm family with harmonious atmosphere. From the beginning that I join the team, I deeply felt the friendship and unity, especially our leadership was very cordial. All the staff are quite cute and other volunteers are friendly. Everybody is always ready to help others. At the same time, we received many concerns from the central, provincial and municipal leaders. In particular, on September 2, the Accreditation Center carefully arranged a group birthday celebration for me and the other four volunteers in the volunteers' room full of pictures and messages on the wall filled with volunteers. Everyone was singing birthday song, making wishes and blowing candles, which was really meaningful.

S1: 志愿者工作很温暖。从主任到校领导、工作人员和各位带队老师,都非常关心志愿者。这个注册中心像一个温暖的大家庭,十分融洽。从 2015 年加入团队之初,我就深刻感受到了注册中心的友爱和团结,领导很亲切,工作人员很可爱,志愿者小伙伴很友善,大家互帮互助,非常融洽。同时,来自中央、省委、市委的领导也经常关心、慰问我们。特别是 9 月 2 日,注册中心为我和其他 4 位志愿者精心安排了集体生日,在贴满了志愿者照片和留言的志愿者之家中,大家唱着生日歌,一起许愿、吹蜡烛,非常有意义。

2.3.4.2 Semi-structured interview with S2 对 S2 的半结构式访谈

Q1：What are your feelings as a volunteer in the Accreditation Center?

提问 1：作为注册中心的志愿者，你的感受如何？

S2：I think it's interesting and meaningful. Seeing all the G20 Summit participants are wearing the ID badges that are gotten from our center, I was particularly happy and proud.

S2：我觉得特别有趣，也特别有意义。看到所有 G20 峰会参与人员的身份牌都是从注册中心出去的，我心里特高兴。

Q2：What do you think of your volunteer work?

提问 2：你怎么看待你这份志愿者工作？

S2：Registration is a very meticulous job. Only when the tasks such as how to fill in the information and how to pay more attention are well-done, can badge-making steps be more efficient. This experience really helps to improve communication and coordination skills.

S2：注册工作是份很细致的活儿，资料怎么填，哪些细节需要注意，这些工作都到位了，后续的制证工作就高效多了。非常锻炼沟通和协调能力。

Q3：Any impressive thing in your volunteer work?

提问 3：请问工作中有哪些印象深刻的事？

S2：Some foreign guests haven't done the online registration, but on-site registration process is somewhat complicated, so a lot of DAOs almost came to the Accreditation Center every day to register for the delegation. One of them complained that our registration process was too complicated, and then one of the volunteers responded in fluent English immediately——"But we have the best service." Those small interactions between people were interesting which in return gave each other a good memory.

S2：一些外宾之前没有在网上注册，现场注册的流程有些复杂，有好多 DAO 几乎每天都要来注册中心为代表团进行注册，有位 DAO 抱怨道我们的注册流程太复杂了，然后我们边上的志愿者反应非常迅速，用英语打趣道"但我们有最好的服务"。这些人与人之间的有趣互动，反而能给对方留下美好的记忆。

Q4：Could you summarize your volunteer work?

提问 4：你可以总结一下你的这次志愿者工作吗？

S2：Interesting and meaningful. Although our work is a little bit obscure, for me it is really meaningful. Not only did I make some contribution to the G20 Hangzhou Summit as a Hangzhou citizen, but this experience helped me improve a lot.

S2：有意思,有意义。虽然我们的工作属于幕后,比较默默无闻,但是对我来说真的非常有意义。这不仅仅是我作为杭州市民为峰会出了一份力,同时也锻炼了我自己。

2.3.4.3 Semi-structured interview with S3 对 S3 的半结构式访谈

Q1：Please say something about your main work as a G20 volunteer.

提问 1：请谈一谈你作为 G20 峰会志愿者的主要工作。

S3：I was in charge of the on-site accreditation area. Our major work is to help delegates do registration through our internet system.

S3：我主要负责现场注册区,我们的主要工作是帮助代表在网上系统进行注册。

Q2：So what are your feelings about the experience?

提问 2：那你对这次志愿者经历有什么感受?

S3：During the period, I learned a lot. Thanks to the experience, I understand the importance of details, such as preparing forms and related materials in advance, the cooperation between every district. I learned how to implement the latest and up-to-date policies in time and how to interoperate. In a word, I learned too much from the accreditation experience, and this experience is very helpful for my future learning and working.

S3：这段时间我学到很多。感谢这次锻炼,让我理解了细节的重要性。我了解了注册中心各个功能区提前准备表单、相关物资的重要性,各个区之间衔接的重要性;我们学到了如何能够及时地践行最新的政策,如何才能最好地进行信息互通,上传下达。总而言之,此次峰会的注册之行让我有太多的学习与感悟,这些经验对我今后的学习、工作都很有帮助。

S4 到 S5 是世界互联网大会的志愿者。

S4 to S5 are the World Internet Conference volunteers.

2.3.4.4 Semi-structured interview with S4 对 S4 的半结构式访谈

Q1：Please briefly introduce your experience of this volunteer experience.

提问 1: 请先简单介绍一下你的工作。

S4: I was a one-to-one volunteer at the third World Internet Conference. My clientele is a heavyweight—Thomas Sargent, who won the 2011 Nobel Prize in Economics.

S4: 本次世界互联网大会上,我是一对一志愿者。我的服务对象是一位重量级人物——2011 年诺贝尔经济学奖得主,托马斯·萨金特。

Q2: What impressed you during the service?

提问 2: 服务过程中有哪些令你印象深刻的事?

S4: When I met Thomas in Pudong Airport, the kind man said "Hi!" to each staff enthusiastically, as if he had undertaken the task for Sino-American friendship. When he saw some novel things, he would exclaim "Amazing!" just like a baby. What impressed me most was that 73-year-old Thomas still insists on sports. He began to look for gym as soon as he arrived at the hotel.

S4: 从上海浦东机场接到托马斯时,这位和蔼的老人就会与每一名工作人员热情地打招呼,就像承担了中美友谊的工作一样,非常真诚。而从上海到乌镇,托马斯就像个好奇宝宝一样,看到新奇的事物都会惊呼"Amazing!"。印象最深的是,73 岁高龄的托马斯仍坚持运动,一到酒店就开始找健身房。

Q3: What are your feelings as a WIC volunteer?

提问 3: 通过这次的志愿者服务,感受如何?

S4: At first, I was just like a fan looking forward to Thomas' signature. Gradually I calmed down to provide interpreter service for him. In those days, I did realize that the success of "big shot" did not depend on luck, but on the accumulation from life bit by bit. Thomas had an 8-minute speech in a meeting. He had been keeping considering how to speak for these 8 minutes because he wanted to express many points. As to this Nobel Prize winner, even his dedication belongs to the "Nobel Prize" level!

S4: 从想抱起书本求签名,到淡定地提供翻译服务,跟着托马斯的几天中,我深刻认识到"大咖"的成功并非靠运气,而是靠生活中点点滴滴的积累。这次会议中,托马斯有一次演讲,时长 8 分钟,由于想表达的东西较多,他一直在斟酌怎样讲才好。诺贝尔奖得主,连认真都是"诺贝尔奖"级别的!

2.3.4.5 Semi-structured interview with S5 对 S5 的半结构式访谈

Q1: Please briefly introduce your experience of this volunteer experience.

提问 1：请先简单介绍一下你的工作。

S5：Among the World Internet Conference volunteers, I was one of the VVIP one-to-one volunteers. My job is to serve the National Minister of Communications & Tech Department of Sudan, including picking-up in the airport, daily arrangements in the WIC, sending-off and so on.

S5：在这次世界互联网大会的志愿者中，我是 VVIP 一对一志愿者，接待了苏丹通讯和科技部国务部长，我的工作包括接机、在乌镇的日常安排、最后送机等。

Q2：What impressed you during this volunteer service?

提问 2：这次志愿者服务有哪些令你印象深刻的事？

S5：My guest has been in Wuzhen for the longest time, totally five days. Every day, I played the roles as a little entourage, secretary and tour guide. However, because the guest's mother tongue is Arabic and his English is not that fluent, at the beginning, our communication was a little bit difficult. Fortunately, after being used to the Arabian English, I finally overcome it. What impressed me most was that my guest liked to take selfies very much, so he often took pictures with me and cheerfully send to me.

S5：我的嘉宾在乌镇待的时间最长，整整五天，我每天都是集"小跟班＋秘书＋导游"于一身，因为嘉宾的母语是阿拉伯语，英语也不是特别好，所以一开始沟通有点困难，但是习惯了之后交流还是无障碍的。印象特别深的是，嘉宾特别喜欢自拍，经常要跟我拍照，然后很开心地发给我。

Q3：What are your feelings as a WIC volunteer?

提问 3：对于这次志愿者服务，你有什么感受？

S5：Everyday my guest often asked me "Where are you?" "How are you?" In fact, I was a little afraid to hear such questions in the begining, but later I felt that they brought me a sense of accomplishment of being needed.

S5：嘉宾每天最喜欢问我的就是"Where are you?" "How are you?"，其实一开始我比较害怕听到这样的话，但后来感觉自己这么被需要，还是有点成就感的。

Q4：What do you think as a volunteer for the WIC are there anything needed to be improved?

提问 4：你觉得作为互联网大会的陪同志愿者，有哪些需要改进的或者不足的地方?

S5： I think the overall volunteer task arrangement is still quite proper. If there is anything to be improved, for example, the information transmission is not timely. The case was that one volunteer was informed of the picking-up task until almost the midnight that day, which nearly ruined the picking-up task. And the information was not updated in time, although my guest is VVIP, his name was at the same time also in the list of ordinary foreign guests. So my guest often received text messages or e-mails from other groups of volunteers, which was quite confusing for them.

S5： 我觉得整体的志愿者任务安排还是非常到位的。但也有需要改进的地方,比如说,信息传递不及时,有志愿者第二天清晨要接机,但是几乎是在前一晚半夜 12 点才接到通知,差一点要耽误接机任务。信息更新不及时,我的嘉宾其实是 VVIP,但是他的名字也在普通境外嘉宾组,所以嘉宾经常接到其他组志愿者的联系短信或邮件,这就造成了混乱。

Q5： As a volunteer in the conference, what do you think when you encounter these problems?

提问 5： 作为会务志愿者,你觉得遇到这些问题的时候,应该怎么办?

S5： I think as a volunteer, firstly, obey the arrangements from the organizing committee. In the face of difficulties, communication is very important as we need timely communication to solve the problem. I think as a one-to-one volunteer, in addition to nurturing the capacity for foreign affairs and language skills, our coordination and communication skills are also enhanced.

S5： 我觉得作为志愿者首先要服从,服从大会安排。在遇到困难的时候要及时沟通解决,所以我认为沟通是非常重要的。我觉得作为一名一对一志愿者,除了锻炼了志愿者的外事和语言能力,还增强了协调和沟通能力。

2.3.5 Extensive Links 拓展链接

Volunteer Training Course
志愿者培训课程

Since LICs need a lot of high-quality volunteers, in terms of the commonality of volunteer service and the individuality of each different meeting, volunteer training is inevitable. During the author's one-year temporary post in the municipal government, one of the main tasks is participating in the selection and training of university volunteers for the G20 Hangzhou Summit, which enabled the author to accumulate relatively more theoretical study and practical experience in this area. Normally the general training of volunteers includes the training from three aspects: spiritual outlook, visual image, and behavior regulations.

既然大型国际会议需要大量的优秀志愿者,那么针对志愿服务的共性和每场会议的个性,志愿者培训也是必不可少的。笔者在一年的市政机关挂职经历中,参与的主要任务之一就是 G20 杭州峰会高校志愿者的选拔和培训,在这一方面积累了较多的理论学习和实践经验。通常,志愿者通用培训包括志愿者精神风貌、视觉形象和行为规范三个方面的培训。

(1)Spiritual outlook 精神风貌

Spiritual outlook refers to the spiritual style, appearance and status, which is a kind of impression from the ideological level. From the perspective of etiquette, it is the spirit of "dedication, love, mutual aid and progress" advocated among volunteers that precisely reflects their respect, humility and kindness towards others and the society.

精神风貌指的是精神层面的风格、面貌、状态,是一种意识形态层面的印象。从礼仪角度来看,志愿者倡导的"奉献、友爱、互助、进步"的精神,恰恰体现出对他人、对社会的恭敬、谦让、仁爱之心。

Volunteers for the G20 Summit not only represent themselves, but also all the university students in Hangzhou or even Zhejiang Province and all Chinese people. They not only represent the citizens' individual qualities to the world, but also represent Hangzhou as an outstanding place with many talents and China as a country of power and inclusiveness.

G20 峰会的志愿者不仅代表了个人,也代表着杭州和浙江高校的大学生,更代表着中国人民。他们不仅向世界展示了中国公民的个体素养,也是向世界展示杭州的人杰地灵,更是向世界展示我大国的气度与风范。

(2)Visual image 视觉形象

Volunteers' visual image mainly includes three aspects: appearance, posture and manners. Teachers and students for the training can embark on these three aspects so as to enhance the visual image of volunteers.

志愿者视觉形象主要包括仪容、仪表和仪态三个方面,培训教师和学生都可以从这三个方面入手,从而提升志愿者的视觉形象。

In terms of appearance, the six words—concise, generous, elegant, fresh, clean and neat—have quite well summarized the principles of volunteers' appearance standards. A smile and an eye contact turn to be the windows to reflect appearance; while posture mainly focuses on clothes. Posture is a kind of mood as well as a kind of power. It's about bringing others aesthetic joys at the same time with self-beauty-appreciation; manners refer to the behavior and its ways, including standing, sitting, walking and bowing, etc. As to bowing, for example, in the face of guests, volunteers should firstly stand to attention and then bend forward upper body from the waist. Male volunteers put two hands on the sides of their bodies while females put two hands together in front of the body. Along with the body bending down, two hands are leaning down gradually towards the direction of the knee.

在仪容方面,简洁、大方、端庄、清爽、干净、整齐这 12 字原则很好地概括了志愿者的仪容标准。一个微笑和一个眼神都是仪容的体现窗口。仪表则主要注重衣着。仪表是一种心情,是一种力量,是在自己审视美的同时,也让别人欣赏美。仪态指举止和做派,包括站姿、坐姿、走姿和鞠躬礼等。比如在鞠躬礼上,面对客人,立正站好,保持身体端正,由腰开始的上身向前弯曲。男性双手放在身体两侧,女性双手合起放在身体前面。随着身体向下弯曲,双手逐渐向下,朝膝盖方向下垂。

(3)Behaviour regulations 行为规范

What kind of behaviors are under volunteers' behavior regulations? What are the specific regulations for each behavior? This is the part with the richest content in the training. First of all, the behaviors under volunteers' behavior regulations are shown in the following figure:

志愿者的行为规范具体规范了哪些行为? 每项行为又具体有哪些规范? 这是培训中内容最多的一块。首先,志愿者行为规范具体规范的行为如下图所示:

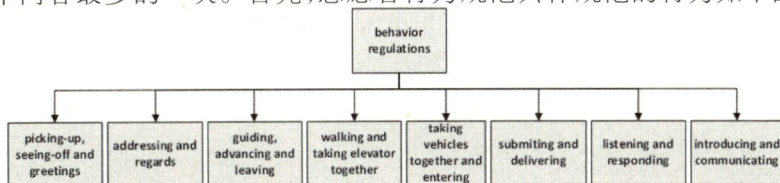

Figure 2-9 Behaviors under Volunteers' Behavior Regulations

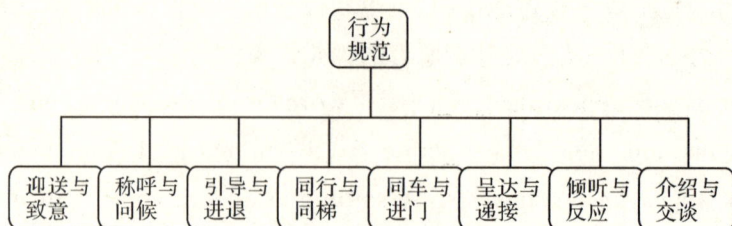

图 2-9 志愿者行为规范具体规范的行为

Secondly, each behavior has its specific regulations. As to the picking-up and seeing-off behavior and the greeting behavior, decent gestures, active services with smiles, politeness, and patient guidance are all necessary. "Three Voices" as welcome voice, responding voice and seeing-off voice should be followed. "Four Distances" as intimate distance, social distance, etiquette distance and public distance should be mastered. While greeting, it calls for natural expression and sincere regards. Greeting forms include nodding, hands shaking, bowing, hugging, kissing, etc. (nodding and bowing are most commonly used). Please do not be too casual with chatting or laughing and do not be cold or turn a blind eye.

其次,每项行为都有它具体的规范。如迎送与致意时要求举止得体、主动服务、微笑服务、文明有礼、耐心引导。做到"三声":来有迎声、问有答声、走有送声。掌握"四距离":亲密距离、社交距离、礼仪距离、公共距离。而致意时则要求表情自然、真诚亲切。形式有点头、握手、鞠躬、拥抱、亲吻等(点头、鞠躬最为常用)。切忌随意、闲聊、嬉笑、冷漠、视而不见。

If readers are interested in participating in volunteer activities of Hangzhou or Zhejiang Province, or if you want to know more about volunteering information, Please refer to the following links below:

如果读者有兴趣参与杭州或浙江省的志愿活动,或者想了解更多志愿服务的信息,可以关注以下网址和公众号:

Hangzhou Volunteer 志愿杭州(www.hzva.org/)

Zhejiang Province Volunteer Information System 浙江省志愿服务信息系统(http://zj.zhiyuanyun.com/)

WeChat Public Account:Volunteer Group

微信公众号:志愿汇

2.4 Internationalization of Hotels
酒店的国际化建设

2.4.1 Brief Introduction 简介

In Maslow's hierarchy of needs, at the bottom of human demand is the physiological needs, including basic necessities of life. As an essential assurance of food and shelter for LICs, the internationalization of hotels has largely influenced the ability of a city to host LICs. In view of the G20 Hangzhou Summit, in the preparatory stage of the Summit, Hangzhou government not only motivated hotel towards the high-end and international goals in the facilities, hotel view and quality of service, but also newly opened several hotels in 2016 in line with the reception specifications. In 2015, the five-star or luxury hotels in Hangzhou up to the international standards were not sufficient to meet the needs of a LIC. Hangzhou Diaoyutai Hotel is one of the hotels opened in August 16, 2016.

在马斯洛需求层次理论里面,人类最底层的需求为生理需求,其中就包括衣食住行。作为大型国际会议的必备食住保障,酒店的国际化建设很大程度上影响了一个城市举办大型国际会议的能力。以 G20 杭州峰会为例,杭州的酒店在峰会筹备阶段不仅在设施、景观和服务质量上朝着高端与国际化的目标迈进,而且由于 2015 年杭州符合接待国际会议标准的五星级或者豪华型酒店数量难以满足一个大型国际会议的需求,杭州于 2016 年新开业了部分符合接待规格的酒店。2016 年 8 月 16 日开业的杭州泛海钓鱼台酒店就是其中一个。

Therefore, a LIC is a major event in the political and economic fields of the country. On the other hand, for the tourism service in Hangzhou and even throughout Zhejiang Province, it helps the transformation of tourism and the upgrading of internationalization. Then in order to provide "safe, healthy, comfortable, convenient" reception service for the delegates and media reporters all around the world, how do the hotel and the government work together to promote the hotel's internal and external image for further internationalization?

因此,大型国际会议不仅是国家政治、经济领域的一项大事,对于杭州乃至整个浙江省来说,将有助于其旅游业的转型升级和国际化水平的提升。那么为了给各代表团参会人员和各国媒体记者提供"安全、卫生、舒适、便利"的酒店接待服务,酒店和政府该如何协同合作,促进酒店内外兼修,从而开展好国际化建设呢?

2.4.1.1 Basic facilities 基础保障方面

Basic facilities are needed by each hotel. But for the hotels requiring internationalization, it is harsher and any break-down is not allowed. After the upgrading, the hotels had completed the hardware renovation work and applied for acceptance approval by the end of June, 2016.

虽然每个酒店都需要基础保障,但对有国际化需求的酒店来说,要求更加苛刻且不能出故障。经提升改造的 G20 接待酒店,于 2016 年 6 月底前完成了硬件设施改造工作,并抓紧进行验收审批。

These hardware facilities include strengthening the daily inspection and maintenance of the elevators, air conditioners and other facilities; setting central air conditioning temperature during the Summit to 24℃ which meets the international practice of human comfort; equipment inspectors being 24 hours on standby during the summit; examining and maintaining the hotel internal water supply facilities comprehensively and strengthening the safety of reservoirs; strengthening safety management of electronic power, including optimizing the line configuration, strengthening maintenance, examining electrical equipment comprehensively, and establishing circuit protection contingency plans; strengthening the daily inspection and maintenance of natural gas equipment to ensure uninterrupted gas supply (The hotels with the transformation of engineering conditions should implement a two-way gas supply).

这些硬件设施工作包括加强电梯、空调等设施设备的日常检查维护;中央空调制冷温度在峰会期间可设定为符合国际惯例的人体舒适温度(24℃);设备维检人员在峰会期间实行 24 小时待命;全面检修酒店内部供水设施,加强蓄水池安全监管;加强电力安全管理,优化线路配置,强化线路维护,并全面检修电器设备,建立电路保障应急预案;加强天然气设备的日常检查维护,确保不间断用气(具备改造工程条件的宾馆应实行双路供气)。

In addition, the hotels which have the summit reception mission must close the tourism reservation during the Summit. For example:

G20 Reception Period:August 27 to September 6;

B20 Reception Period:September 1 to 5;

Media Reception Period:September 1 to 6.

此外,有接待任务的酒店关闭所有会议期间时段内的(游客)预订通道,比如:

G20 接待酒店:8 月 27 日至 9 月 6 日;

B20 接待酒店:9 月 1 日至 5 日;

媒体接待酒店:9 月 1 日至 6 日。

2.4.1.2 Communication 通信通讯方面

As to the reception of foreign guests, network problems of foreign communication equipment make it much more complicated than the reception of domestic ones. This requires the hotels to improve WiFi hardware facilities both to meet the safety requirements and to achieve functions such as the whole network roaming services, private network services. Hotels' internal communication facilities should implement dual routing and coordinate with the operators of indoor wireless signal distribution system transformation. In the hotels, especially reception hotels for media staff, every interior area should have fast internet access conditions to ensure smooth transmission of audio and video information.

酒店接待外国嘉宾,就会涉及国外的通信设备联网问题,相对来说比接待国内客人要复杂得多。这就要求酒店改造 WiFi 硬件设施,确保既符合安全要求,又具备全网漫游、专网服务等功能。宾馆内部通信设施要实行双路由,并配合运营商进行无线信号室内分布系统改造。接待酒店尤其是媒体接待酒店内部各区域应具备快速上网条件,确保音频、视频信息传输畅通。

2.4.1.3 Internal environment 内部环境方面

In addition to basic needs like infrastructure support and communication, hotels' international construction also means to optimize the hotel interior decoration and furnishings, so as to become in harmony with the overall style of the hotel. After we confirm who are the exact guests to serve, internal environment is expected to meet their individual requirements, in particular, to take the cultural differences into account.

除了基础保障和通信等基本需求,酒店的国际化建设还意味着要优化宾馆内部装饰与陈设,使之与宾馆整体风格相协调。接待对象确定后,还要满足个性化的要求,特别要考虑文化风俗差异。

On the other hand, as people's awareness of environment is becoming higher, indoor air quality of the hotels should be in accordance with international environmental monitoring standards. Don't spray air purification auxiliary products with strong fragrance, or place plants with strong smells. Bathroom odor should be removed and the ground be non-slipped.

另一方面,随着人们对环境的意识越来越高,宾馆室内空气质量要达到国际环保监测标准,不得喷洒香味浓郁的空气净化辅助产品,或放置有气味的植物。卫生间不能有异味,地面做好防滑处理。

2.4.1.4 Food and sanitation 食品及卫生方面

By the end of June 2016, the summit reception hotels had completed the upgrading of kitchen equipment and built "sunshine kitchen." Food service management had reached A-level. Similarly, to achieve hotels' internationalization, it is also necessary to strengthen the catering practitioners' operating skills training and implement strictly the management system such as morning inspection by staff, certificate or receipt examination of food origin, and complying with food security regulations. The summit reception hotels provide 24 hour catering service (including room service), all kinds of meals, refreshments, coffee, drinks, etc., which are required to meet the international high quality service standards.

2016 年 6 月底前,峰会接待酒店完成了厨房硬件设备的改造升级,建成了"阳光厨房",餐饮服务量化分级管理达到 A 级。同样,酒店的国际化建设也需要加强餐饮从业人员操作技能培训,严格执行员工晨检、食品来源索证索票等管理制度及食品安全操作规范。提供 24 小时餐饮服务(包括客房送餐服务),各式餐食、茶点、咖啡、饮品等均须符合国际惯例的高品质服务水准。

The hotels should fully understand the customs of different countries, for instance, to provide Muslims with halal meals.

特别是要了解不同国家的餐饮习惯习俗,比如针对穆斯林贵宾提供清真餐食服务。

2.4.1.5 Security 安全保卫方面

Although the LIC is often accompanied by external equipment of security, the hotel managers should participate in the whole processes of conference service, specifically in charge of coordination of hotel rooms, meals, meetings, entertainment, finance, transportation, logistics, power security, medical, hotel security and other aspects. At the same time, the hotels should cooperate with the security department to do personnel's background review and accreditation; strictly implement the real-name registration system. For example, before the Summit, the presidential suite of the G20 reception hotels must be strictly in accordance with the regulations of security and put system of "the certain person in charge and for report" into practice.

虽然大型国际会议常常伴随着外部安保的配备,但酒店经理需全程跟会,具体协调酒店房、餐、会议、娱乐、财务、交通、后勤、动力保卫、医疗、酒店安全保卫等方面的工作。同时,酒店要配合安保部门做好从业人员背景审查和认证工作。严格落实入住酒店人员实名登记制度。比如 G20 接待酒店的总统套房,在峰会前对外接待必须严格按照安保规定,实行专人、专管、专报制度。

2.4.1.6 Staff 从业人员方面

Language plays a vital part in hotels' international construction. To carry out foreign languages training is a progressive process, which requires the hotels to plan and adhere. Besides, foreign reception etiquette, service standards, service skills and other training are also essential. The confidentiality of many international meetings determines the hotels to strengthen the staff confidential training and to sign a letter of confidentiality. The staff member shall not leak guests' information before the reception task is completed, or shall not post it on the Internet, WeChat, microblog and other public platforms.

语言交流是酒店国际化建设里面至关重要的一环。开展服务人员外语水平培训是一个渐进的过程,需要酒店有筹划地坚持进行。此外,涉外接待礼仪、服务规范、服务技能等培训也必不可少。许多国际会议的保密性质决定了酒店要加强工作人员保密培训,签订保密承诺书。工作人员不得在接待任务完成前外传接待对象、接待方案信息,不得在互联网、微信、微博及其他公共平台上发布信息。

2.4.1.7 Personalized services 个性化服务方面

Personalized services needed during hotels' internationalization are worthy of improving, such as setting up a specialized service counter, providing 24-hour service for international settlement, international payment, exchange, international postal services, etc. According to the relevant regulations, the hotels should have the access to foreign television channels in order to meet the various television demands among foreign guests of different nationality.

酒店国际化需要的许多个性化服务值得完善。比如设置专门的服务柜台,负责 24 小时提供国际结算、国际支付、外币兑换、国际邮政等服务。按有关规定,开通境外电视频道,满足不同国籍的外宾收看不同的电视节目的需求。

What we have to discuss about personalized services is respecting the guests' religious beliefs. For example, Muslims need a public pray room and it is better to provide a small carpet in Muslims' own room and mark the direction to the public pray room. After confirming which guest group to serve, the hotels should spare no effort to meet their reasonable individual needs in the business negotiations.

个性化服务里不得不提的是尊重宾客的宗教信仰。举例来说,为穆斯林贵宾提供公共祈祷室,也可以在其房间提供小地毯并标注去公共祈祷室的方向。接待对象确定后,在商务洽谈中应尽最大努力满足对方提出的合理的个性化需求。

Hotel stores can sell tourist souvenirs of local and travel characteristics goods other than counterfeit and shoddy goods.

酒店商店可出售有当地特色的旅游纪念品及旅行用品,不得出售假冒、伪劣商品。

2.4.2 Words, Phrases and Sentences 词汇、短语和例句

Maslow's hierarchy of needs 马斯洛需求层次理论

an essential assurance of food and shelter 食住的必备保障

the transformation of tourism and the upgrading of internationalization
旅游业的转型升级和国际化水平的提升

hardware renovation work 硬件设施改造工作

optimize the hotel interior decoration and furnishings 优化宾馆内部装饰与陈设

become in harmony with 与……相协调

coordination of hotel rooms 协调酒店房间

service standard 服务规范

confidentiality 机密性

sign a letter of confidentiality 签订保密承诺书

personnel's background review and accreditation
从业人员背景审查和认证工作

real-name registration system 实名登记制度

provide a small carpet 提供小地毯

counterfeit and shoddy goods 假冒、伪劣商品

(1) The hotels should fully understand the customs of different countries, for instance, to provide Muslims with halal meals.

特别是要了解不同国家的餐饮习惯习俗,比如针对穆斯林贵宾提供清真餐食服务。

(2) For example, before the Summit, the presidential suite of the G20 reception hotels must be strictly in accordance with the provisions of security and put system of "the certain person for charge and report" into practice.

比如 G20 接待酒店的总统套房,在峰会前对外接待必须严格按照安保规定,实行专人、专管、专报制度。

(3) To carry out foreign languages training is a progressive process, which requires the hotel to plan and adhere.

开展服务人员外语水平培训是一个渐进的过程,需要酒店有筹划地坚持进行。

(4) The staff member shall not leak guests' information before the reception task is completed, or shall not post it on the Internet, WeChat,

microblog and other public platforms.

工作人员不得在接待任务完成前外传接待对象、接待方案信息,不得在互联网、微信、微博及其他公共平台上发布信息。

(5) Personalized services needed during hotels' internationalization are worthy of improving, such as setting up a specialized service counter, providing 24-hour service for international settlement, international payment, exchange, international postal services, etc.

酒店国际化需要的许多个性化服务值得完善。比如设置专门的服务柜台,负责 24 小时提供国际结算、国际支付、外币兑换、国际邮政等服务。

(6) What we have to discuss about personalized services is respecting the guests' religious beliefs.

个性化服务里不得不提的是尊重宾客的宗教信仰。

2.4.3 Situation Practice 情景演练

How to Provide Better Laundry Service in Housekeeping Department
客房部如何提供更优的洗衣服务

Housekeeping Department in your hotel has received many customers' calls for laundry service since there is a Large International Conference in the city these days. Two following factors have contributed to the challenges in front of the staff there. First and foremost, it is relatively difficult for the staff and the customers to communicate with each other. Secondly, fulfilling so many laundry orders with high efficiency and low chances of mistakes has obviously become a challenge as well.

最近,一个大型国际会议在你们城市举行,因此你所在的酒店客房部收到了许多入住代表关于洗衣服务的电话。由于以下两个因素,客房部的员工面临着挑战。首先最重要的是,员工和客人交流起来较为困难。其次,高效而又少失误地完成这么多洗衣服务显然是另一个挑战。

Please read the above situation description carefully and get to know some useful oral expressions of laundry service from the following dialogues. In this case, G stands for the guest, R stands for the registration desk, while S stands for the staff of Housekeeping Department.

请仔细阅读上面这一情景描述,并从下面的对话里学习一些洗衣服务中常用的口语表达。其中,G 表示客人,R 表示登记员,S 表示客房部员工。

Dialogue 1

G： Hello! This is room 4208. Can I have laundry service?

R： Yes, please. Could you fill in the laundry list in your room and our housekeeper will come to your room soon to pick up the list and your laundry.

G： OK, thanks. I'll do that.

(Doorbell)

S： Good morning, sir! May I collect your laundry and the list now?

G： Sure. But before you leave, I wanna confirm my laundry list with you. That is, three shirts, one pair of suit pants and one sweater. Is it OK?

S： Yes, sir. We just checked together. It's all right.

G： Ah... By the way, make sure the sweater won't get shrunk after the laundry 'cause it's really of good quality.

S： Don't worry, sir. We'll take care of it.

G： Good. Thanks! See you!

S： See you! Have a nice day, sir!

客人：你好! 这里是 4208 房间。我可以叫洗衣服务吗?

登记员：可以。您可以填好房间里的洗衣单,我们客房部的洗衣工很快就会去您的房间取洗衣单和要洗的衣物。

客人：好的,谢谢。我会填好的。

(门铃)

洗衣员：先生,早上好! 我可以取您要洗的衣物和填好的洗衣单吗?

客人：当然。但在你拿走之前,我和你核对一下清单上这些衣服是不是都在这儿了。三件衬衫,一条西装裤,一件毛衣,对吧?

洗衣员：是的,先生。我们刚刚一起核对了,都在这了。

客人：对了,顺便说一下。你们洗的时候确保这个毛衣不能缩水哦,因为它质量真的不错。

洗衣员：别担心,先生。我们会注意的。

客人：好的,谢谢! 再见!

洗衣员：再见! 祝您今天愉快,先生!

Dialogue 2

G: Hi! This is room 3618. It's 8:00 pm already and I haven't received my laundry yet. Where's my laundry?

R: When did you send it?

G: This morning.

R: I'll check with Laundry Service to see if your laundry has come back yet. I'll call you back shortly.

R: Hello, Mr. Wohler? This is Housekeeping Department. The Laundry Service is delivering the laundry right now. They will come to your room very soon. We are sorry for the delay.

客人: 你好！这是 3618 房间。已经晚上 8 点了,我还没有收到洗好的衣服。我的衣服在哪儿呢？

登记员: 您是什么时候送洗的？

客人: 今天早晨。

登记员: 我问一下洗衣部您的衣服是否已经洗好了,过一会儿我再给您回电话。

登记员: 您好,是维勒先生吗？我是客房部。洗衣服务员现在正在送洗熨好的衣服。他们马上去您的房间。非常抱歉衣服送晚了。

Dialogue 3

G: I've several complaints here. Firstly, I'm missing a skirt. I sent two skirts in the laundry yesterday and only one came back. Secondly, I need to do laundry today and I called before, but the Laundry Service never picked up my laundry today.

R: I'm very sorry. Is this room 8117? As to your missing skirt, I'll check with the Laundry Service about it and call you back soon. As to the delay today, it's because we've received too many orders from too many customers. But don't worry, I'll send somebody to your room right away to pick it up.

G: But I need these skirts for tomorrow! Please check as soon as possible, OK?

R: OK! I'm terribly sorry for the inconvenience.

(Doorbell)

S: Good afternoon, Madam! I'm from the Laundry Service and this is your missing skirt. It's already washed and dried. Sorry for the inconvenience. Here you are.

G: OK. Never mind. Anyway, it's clean and back to me.

S: Thanks for your understanding. Here is the IOU slip for the missing piece. Please sign here to make sure you received it now. Thanks very much!

G: Here? Done!

客人: 我有几个事情要投诉一下。首先,我少了条裙子。昨天我送洗了两条裙子,今天只拿回来一条。第二,我今天也有衣物送洗,我打了电话但洗衣部今天一直没有来取我的衣服。

登记员:非常对不起。是 8117 房间吗? 关于您未送回的裙子,我和洗衣部确认一下给您回复。关于今天要送洗的衣物,因为我们今天收到了太多客人的洗衣订单,但请您放心,我立即派人到您房间去取。

旅客: 可是明天我需要这些裙子! 请你马上确认,好吗?

登记员:没问题! 对于给您带来的不便,我深感抱歉。

(门铃)

洗衣员:女士,下午好! 我是洗衣部的,这是未送回的裙子,已经洗好晾干了。对于给您带来的不便,我们深感抱歉。您拿好。

客人:好的。没关系。不管怎样,洗好送回来了。

洗衣员:谢谢理解。这是欠衣单,麻烦您在这边签个字,确认这条裙子您收到了。谢谢!

客人:这里吗? 签好了!

2.4.4 Hotel Staff Interview 酒店人员访谈

This section follows the research methods used in "Preparation Work of Conferences" of the second chapter, that is, semi-structured interview. The interviews are conducted to one hotel's staff for a president group's reception during the Hangzhou Summit. In view of the privacy requirements by the interviewee, the following D is used to refer to the interviewee here.

本小节沿用第二章"会议筹备工作"里面的研究方法,即半结构式访谈,对杭州峰会某总统团接待酒店的酒店员工开展了相关访谈。鉴于访谈对象的个人隐私要求,以下用 D 来指称此位受访者。

Q1: Hello! Our interview is mainly intended for the preparation of LICs.

As a hotel receptionist and after experiencing the reception of the G20 Summit, what are the differences compared with other meetings in terms of difficulty, intensity and steps? For example, provincial or municipal level meetings or even smaller international conferences?

提问 1: 您好! 我们这次访谈主要是针对大型国际会议的筹备工作。那么您作为酒店接待人员,在经历了 G20 峰会这样的大型国际会议的接待工作之后,觉得它和准备其他会议在难度、强度和步骤上有什么明显区别? 比如和省级、市级会议或者小型的国际会议相比,在这些方面有什么区别?

D: First of all, as to difficulty, I think that preparing for a LIC is certainly more difficult than for the provincial or municipal level or even smaller international conference. Specifically speaking, it is the language that is the prior difficulty. We, the staff, must pass the first obstacle, that is, the language. Secondly, as to intensity, the large number of participants and teams is also a test for our services, as I am concerned.

D: 首先我觉得难度上,大型国际会议的准备工作肯定比省级、市级和小型国际会议的难度高。具体来说第一个就是语言,我们的服务人员首先要过的是语言这一关。第二个是强度,我觉得国际型会议,它的参与人员和团队数量很大,对我们的服务来说也是一种考验。

Q2: Then I would like to ask, did the hotel really carry out certain language trainings for the hotel reception staff? If yes, how to do it? If the labor force is not sufficient for a big group of delegates, how to solve this problem? Was there anyone recruited from outside to make up the vacancy?

提问 2: 那我想问一下,当时酒店有专门给酒店的接待人员开展语言培训吗? 如果有的话是如何开展的呢? 人手方面不够的话,怎么解决这个问题,是从外面招募吗?

D: The hotel prepared a lot of language training for staff. Before confirming which delegation we are going to serve, we already had English training. After acknowledging Mexico as our guest delegation, we received some basic Spanish training. During the Summit, because of language barrier, we also made use of spare time to learn. We have 24-hour butler service on each floor. Butler of each floor can speak some related foreign language. Those housekeepers who can speak both English and Spanish are on duty in turn.

D：酒店是准备了很多语言培训的,在不确定接待哪个代表团之前,我们开展的是英语培训;在确定接待墨西哥代表团以后,我们接受了一些基础的西班牙语培训。在峰会期间,因为语言上有障碍,我们也在加班加点地学习。我们每个楼层设置了 24 小时的管家式服务。每个楼层的管家都会说相关的语言,还有会说英语和西班牙语的客服服务人员在轮流值班。

Q3： As to hotel reception work of the LIC, do you have any work experience or interesting stories that can be shared here with us?

提问 3：关于大型国际会议的酒店接待工作,你有什么工作经验或者有趣的故事可以在这里和我们分享一下吗?

D： Personally, I think we did lack the reception experience of such a high-level international conference. So in my opinion if we still have the opportunity to undertake a LIC in the future, first of all, we need to start from improving our own professional knowledge. What's more, these international conference reception standards are necessary to master as well. To be frank, we also have a lot of interesting stories from this reception.

D：从我个人来说,我觉得以前这种大型国际会议的接待经历比较少。那么接下来如果继续有机会承接这些大型国际会议的话,我们首先需要从自身开始丰富业务知识,这些国际会议的接待标准我们也要去学习。说实话,在这次接待经历中我们也有许多有趣的故事。

Q4： Yes, before this interview, I was lucky to see a group photo of you and the foreign representatives and leaders, from which I found that they are very easy-going during their stay in the hotel. But in these processes of taking a group photo with the delegates or other contacts with them, are there any etiquette or communicative approach needed to be aware of? Can you tell us something about that?

提问 4：对啊,之前我有幸看到了你与外国代表和领导人的合影,我发现他们在酒店期间都比较随和。你在与代表合影和接触的过程中,有没有什么礼仪要注意呢,或者有什么交际方式,可以给我们讲讲吗?

D： Yeah, that's what I want to say. We received Mexico Delegation and WBG (World Bank Group). We felt very nervous at the very beginning because it is the reception task for heads of state. But in the course of subsequent contact, we found that both the delegates and leaders are very easy-going. Once

I was taking selfies alone, a high-level delegate even came initiatively and took a photo with me friendly.

D:对,这就是我想说的。我们接待的是墨西哥总统团和世界银行团队,毕竟是一个元首级的接待任务,我们一开始接到这个任务的时候是非常紧张的。但是在后来接触的过程中,我们发现他们无论是代表还是领导人都很随和。有一次我在自拍,有一个较高级别的代表竟然主动过来友好地和我一起拍照。

Besides, we also had the opportunity to take a photo with the first lady of Mexico. The process was also very interesting. We were relatively nervous, thinking whether it's improper to invite the first lady to take a photo with us. However, since we had much contact with the first lady's entourage on some working issues, we just asked one of her staff. To our surprise, he immediately replied yes though we had to wait for a while as the first lady would come over to take pictures with us in a few minutes.

我们也有幸和墨西哥第一夫人拍了合影。这个合影的来历也非常有意思。我们是比较紧张的,担心邀请第一夫人拍合照会不会有所不妥。好在我们和第一夫人身边的工作人员接触得多,于是我们向她身边的工作人员询问,他马上回复说可以的,你们就在这边等一会儿,待会儿夫人过来可以和大家合影。

There's another interesting story. Mexico is rich in tequila and one of the staff brought two boxes of tequila with him and there were some small accidents in the airport customs because of that. He was also quite willing to share with us. It was from then on that we knew tequila is originated from Mexico.

另外还有一个有趣的回忆。墨西哥是盛产龙舌兰的国家,其中一个工作人员带了两箱龙舌兰过来,听说过海关的时候还发生了一些小插曲。这个工作人员也很愿意把他带来的特产和我们一起分享。我们也是从那时候才知道龙舌兰的原产国是墨西哥。

However, because of the language barrier, he didn't talk with all of our colleagues. Still he had a lot of communication with our English and Spanish interpreters because he needed us to interpret during his whole stay in the hotel. Therefore, he sent us tequila as a gift to show his gratitude, so did some other delegates. As far as I'm concerned, our staff in the hotel are very lucky as you can get to know these delegates in a more relaxed atmosphere outside the conference.

但因为语言障碍,他并不是和我们所有工作人员都有交流,而是和我们的英语、西班牙语的翻译交流得多。因为他在酒店这几天的吃喝住行都需要翻译,所以他也把这些礼物送给我们表示感谢,其他的一些代表也类似。所以我觉得我们酒店的工作人员是非常幸运的,因为你可以了解代表们在开会之余比较轻松的状态。

Q5：In different preparation stages of the conference reception, such as the early stage, interim and the later one, in your mind what are the key points for the hotel in different stages? Would you like to talk a bit according to what you have experienced or learned?

提问 5：你觉得,在会议接待准备的不同阶段,比如前期、中期、后期,酒店工作的重点有什么不同吗？你可以就你经历的或者了解到的谈一谈吗？

D：Uh... In the early stage, the requirement on the staff was to upgrade our own professional abilities. As to front office staff, you must master skills of dealing with express deliveries, and know how to exchange foreign currency. Secondly, in the middle when we were informed of the specific country to serve, we must understand the corresponding national culture, etiquette, and their diet habits.

D：呃……前期的话,对工作人员的要求就是你要提升自身的业务能力。对前厅部工作人员来说,你要掌握快件收寄能力,了解外币兑换。第二,在中期的话,我们确定了接待哪个国家以后,那相应国家的文化、礼仪,还有他们的饮食作息习惯,你都需要去了解。

In addition, I think the most important thing in the middle preparatory stage was to learn foreign languages. If Hangzhou wants to continue to host these LICs, for all staff, especially in the hotel, there is still a long way to go to enhance the language. Actually, all of the participants stay in the hotel for the majority of their time since they need communication as well as diet and accommodation. They need supports from the hotel staff for all these aspects. If the interpreting task relies on only part of the staff, such as the Butler of each floor in every building during the meeting, our work is stressful and intensive. To be honest, this situation is not proper for our work to be carried out smoothly.

然后,在筹备的中期,我觉得最重要的一点就是要过语言关。因为杭州以后想要继续承办这些大型国际会议的话,对所有工作人员尤其是酒店工作人员来说,语言这一块要提升的空间还很大。其实,所有参会人员在酒店待的时间是最多的,因为他们需要沟通,需要解决衣食住行。他们在这些方面都需要酒店工作人员的支持。在语言上如果只靠部分人,比如说这次会议我们大部分的翻译工作是落在我们每栋楼每层的管家身上的,那我们几个人的工作压力和工作强度是非常大的,而且说实话,这对工作的展开都是不利的。

For example, if a guest wants to do the laundry, he will turn to the Housekeeping Department. If no one there could understand basic English or Spanish or they want to find others to translate for them, first of all, it will cost longer time, then the guest's satisfaction will be lowered. This situation usually won't or less frequently appear in provincial or municipal meetings or smaller international conferences.

比如说客人要洗件衣服,那他找到客房部,客房部如果连这样一个基本的要求都听不懂,或者想要去寻求其他人翻译的话,那么首先它的持续时间会比较长,其次宾客的满意度就会比较低。这种情况在省级、市级会议和小型国际会议里就不会出现或较少出现。

As an essential reception part of the international meetings, it is a pity that our quality of service is weakened simply because of communication problems in the hotels. But at present the hotel industry generally has such a problem. Maybe the recruitment requirements are not relatively high. So the staff's English ability, especially like our Security Department, Housekeeping Department or Catering Department, is very weak.

酒店作为国际型接待会议中必不可少的一个地方,如果因为沟通上的问题就拉低了服务标准的话,其实非常可惜啊!但是目前酒店行业就是存在这样的问题。可能我们酒店行业的许多部门,相对来说入职的要求并不是很高,所以人员在语言方面,尤其像安保部门、客房部门或者餐饮部门的英语水平,都是非常非常薄弱的。

Q6: So during the whole process of preparation, what are your deepest feelings from the perspective of your work? Can it provide any reference for the future large-scale international activities in Zhejiang Province?

提问 6:那么整个筹备过程中,从您的工作视角来看,您最深的感受是什么?可以为下次我们浙江省举办大型国际活动提供什么借鉴?

D: We prepared a lot of things and searched about the guest country's customs online in advance. But you will find that when the guests arrived, their actual habits are different from what we searched online, so the hotel ought to make adjustments timely.

D: 我们之前准备了很多东西,也在网上搜索了宾客国家的风俗习惯。但当客人来了以后,你会发现他们真正的习惯和网上搜索到的是不一样的,那么酒店就要及时做出调整。

For example, you may have heard that Mexico's daily habits are not the same as ours. Originally we estimated it's only slightly different, but later we found it quite different from ours. So the hotel need adapt to the guests' time: their breakfast time is 10 am to 11 am, lunch time is 2 pm to 3 pm, and dinner time is 11 pm or even later. So if in the future, to hold such a LIC, in addition to online research to understand the customs of different countries, hotels also should accumulate experience in the practice and cope with it flexibly in the actual practice.

比如,大家可能听说过墨西哥的作息习惯和我们不大一样,我们原先预估只是稍微不同,但后来发现有很大不同,所以酒店需要适应客人的作息并及时做出应对。他们的早饭时间是 10 点到 11 点,中饭时间是 14 点到 15 点,晚饭时间已经 23 点甚至凌晨以后了。所以以后再举办这样的大型国际会议的话,酒店除了网上搜索,了解不同国家的风俗习惯,还要在实践中积累经验,在实战中灵活应对。

Q6: Yes, that's the cultural difference. So I think, you are more fortunate than other hotel staff. Due to your advantages of language skills and cultural knowledge, you can communicate with them more smoothly.

提问 4:是的,这个就是文化差异了啊。所以我觉得相对来说的话,你还是酒店员工里面比较幸运的,由于语言技能和文化知识上面的优势,可能还比较好跟他们沟通。

D: So as I said before, we cannot waste the guests' time or reduce their satisfaction index just because of language barriers, which is the right point we need to strengthen. In this way, we can ease the pressure of interpreting task of some of our employees.

D: 所以就像我之前说到的,我们不能因为语言障碍耽误客人时间,降低满意指数,这一块是我们亟待加强的。这样一来也可以缓解我们部分员工的翻译压力。

2.4.5 Extensive Links 拓展链接

After the above discussion about hotels' internationalization and the interview with hotel staff with related experiences, here in the extensive links, let's visit with the guests these hotels which have served the leaders and delegates of different countries in LICs.

讲了酒店的国际化建设,采访了有接待经验的酒店员工,下面在拓展链接里,让我们一起过一把大型国际会议的嘉宾瘾,游览一下会议期间各国政要和代表入住的酒店。

Many people invariably think that it is the city's historical heritage and landscape characteristics that make Hangzhou the host city of G20. No matter the poem "The West Lake looks like the fair lady at her best; Whether she is richly adorned or plainly dressed" or another poem "Among all the sights in Jiangnan area, Hangzhou left the deepest impression on me," they both make people yearn for the Summit here. But when it comes to the G20 Hangzhou Summit, many leaders not only praised the taskforce for the effective organizing works, but also showed great interests in the basic necessities of life in Hangzhou, especially the hotels they lived in. As to the hotels where the political leaders of those countries stayed, the heat did not decrease as the end of the meetings. On the contrary, people began to prepare hotels for the following LICs in Hangzhou.

谈及选址在杭州举办 G20 峰会,许多人都不约而同地认为是因为这座城市的历史底蕴和风景特色。无论是"欲把西湖比西子,淡妆浓抹总相宜",还是"忆江南,最忆是杭州",都可以让人向往这里的会议。但若谈及这次 G20 峰会,许多领导人在赞扬筹备办组织工作得力之外,还对杭州的衣食住行,特别是下榻的酒店情有独钟。关于会议期间各国政要住过的酒店,讨论的热度也丝毫未随着会议的结束而减退。相反,人们开始为接下来在杭举办的大型国际会议筹划起来了。

Here are some "specialist" hotels of international reception, now let's take a look at the internationalized style of these hotels.

此处我们整理了部分国际接待"专业户"酒店,下面就让我们来一睹这些酒店的国际范。

2.4.5.1 Hangzhou XIHU State Guesthouse 西湖国宾馆

It seems that XIHU State Guesthouse is the most significant hotel serving the VIP foreign guests in Hangzhou. It served Chairman Mao Zedong in 1953, and from then on, about 40 leaders from all over the world, including President Nixon and President Mandela, stayed in this hotel before. During the G20 Hangzhou Summit, the Xi-Obama meeting was also held in the Guesthouse. XIHU State Guesthouse is said to have the most charming garden in West Lake. It is located in the west of the Lake, and opposite to Su Causeway. Inside the 360 thousand square meters' garden there are bridges over flowing stream and winding paths leading to secluded quiet places. There are rich cultural landscapes which combine Hangzhou's elegance with beauty. When you live in this Guesthouse, you can step out to the courtyard whenever you like, walk or halt to enjoy the special beauty of West Lake without the disturbance of the outside world.

西湖国宾馆大概是整个杭州接待外宾最重要的场所了。从 1953 年毛泽东第一次住进国宾馆一号楼起,西湖国宾馆一共接待了包括尼克松、曼德拉在内的40 余位国家元首及政要。这次 G20,习近平主席与奥巴马总统会晤的"习奥会"就在西湖国宾馆进行。被誉为"西湖第一名园"的西湖国宾馆位于西湖的西面,与苏堤隔水相望。36 万平方米的庭院内小桥流水,曲径通幽,还有丰富的人文景观,完全将杭州的清雅毓秀之美集于一体。如果住在西湖国宾馆,你可以随时走出门外,在庭院内走走停停,既可以避开拥挤的游客人群,又可以感受独特的西湖景致。

As the hotel for the leaders, the service and facilities of the Guesthouse are really beyond expectation. From the waiters' consideration and quality to the bedding articles, food and beverage, the Guesthouse is such a proper choice that you don't need to think too much, instead, you just stay and enjoy yourself.

作为领导人下榻的地方,西湖国宾馆的服务和设施自然没话说。从服务人员的贴心程度和服务素质,到酒店提供的床品、餐饮等来说,入住西湖国宾馆,大概是最不需要想太多的选择吧,只需静静享受就好。

2.4.5.2 JW Marriott Hangzhou 杭州 JW 万豪酒店

While proposing a hotel to a delegation, the preparatory committee of LICs will firstly take into account the matching degree between the hotel and the nationality of the delegation. Recommending their local brand hotels to the delegation is normally the international practice. For example, during G20 Hangzhou Summit, president Obama and the American delegation lived in JW Marriott Hangzhou. While president of France, Holland, and the French delegation lived in Sofitel West Lake Hangzhou as Sofitel is a France-originated brand.

大型国际会议筹备委员会在给代表团建议入住哪家酒店的时候,都会首先考虑到酒店和代表团所属国家的匹配度。按照国际惯例,往往是把属于这个国家本土品牌的酒店推荐给同一个国家的代表团。比如美国本土企业万豪酒店接待的是美国奥巴马访问团,而法国品牌索菲特酒店接待的是法国奥朗德访问团。

As the leading brand in the hotel industry, Marriott achieved more confidence after the acquisition of Starwood Hotels. Facing the high standards and requirements of the American delegation, JW Marriott Hangzhou's cautious and conscientious service and successful completion of the reception, won high praise from the US Ground Army. The following picture shows the Certificate of Appreciation signed by The Liaison Office of White House to JW Marriott Hangzhou.

万豪酒店,作为酒店业界的龙头老大之一,在收购了喜达屋之后更是气场十足。面对高标准、高要求的美国访问团,杭州 JW 万豪兢兢业业,圆满完成了接待任务,受到美国陆军战队的高度赞赏。下图为白宫办公厅联络办公室颁发给杭州 JW 万豪的感谢卡。

Figure 2-10 Certificate of Appreciation of White House to JW Marriott Hangzhou

图 2-10 白宫颁发给杭州 JW 万豪的感谢卡

2.4.5.3 Midtown Shangri-La Hangzhou 杭州城中香格里拉大酒店

The first Shangri-La hotel in Mainland China was opened in Hangzhou in 1984. Each room features French window with a wide West Lake views. The hotel consists of two main buildings and three single villas, offering in total 417 spacious guestrooms and suites. It is well known for excellent environment and high-quality service. The beauty of the West Lake and the high-quality service of Midtown Shangri-La haven't changed for 30 years.

1984 年,中国大陆开的第一家香格里拉大酒店,便坐落于杭州。透过房内的落地窗,西湖美景一览无遗。杭州城中香格里拉大酒店由两栋主楼和三套独立别墅组成,共 417 间客房和套房,以优美迷人的环境及殷勤周到的服务而闻名。30 多年过去了,不变的是西湖的美,还有香格里拉一贯的高品质服务。

Figure 2-11　Midtown Shangri-La Hangzhou
图 2-11　杭州城中香格里拉酒店

2.4.5.4 Sofitel Westlake Hangzhou 杭州索菲特西湖大酒店

The Sofitel Westlake Hangzhou is a hotel managed by Accor Hotels. Many leaders including Holland, the French President, Donald Tusk, the President of the European Council, and Juncker, the President of European Commission, stayed here during the Summit. It owns a unique location by West Lake in city center with easy access to ritzy restaurants and shops in the West Lake shopping center.

杭州索菲特西湖大酒店由法国雅高集团管理,在峰会期间入住该酒店的领导人众多,有法国总统奥朗德、欧洲理事会主席图斯克和欧盟委员会主席容克。它

静驻于西子湖畔,闹市之中。从酒店出发,很快就可以到达西湖天地购物休闲中心的高档商店和餐厅。

The hotel boasts stunning views of the legendary West Lake with cloud-covered lush mountains. The prosperous and unique historical features of Hangzhou interweave in this place.

这里,坐拥露天西湖美景,山色空蒙,青黛含翠;可以饱览绿荫葱葱的城市繁华以及历史温香的独特风情。

2.4.5.5 Huajiashan Resort Hangzhou 杭州花家山庄

Huajiashan Resort Hangzhou is located in the hinterland of West Lake. During the Summit, it served Enrique Peña Nieto, Mexican President, Ms. Christine Lagarde, President of International Monetary Fund, Jacoby, the US Treasury Secretary, and other important guests. It is worth mentioning that in order to prepare the G20 Hangzhou Summit, the resort had beautified its night lighting.

花家山庄位于西湖腹地,在峰会期间,接待了墨西哥总统培尼亚·涅托、国际货币基金组织(IMF)总裁拉加德女士、美国财政部长雅各布卢等重要国际人士。值得一提的是,花家山庄在 G20 杭州峰会举办前,进行了夜景灯光提升工作。

Figure 2-13　Night Scene of Huajiashan Resort

图 2-13　花家山庄夜景

Huajiashan Resort is a villa-style resort and China's former Prime Minister Zhou Enlai visited here before. It is located in the south-end of Yang Gong Causeway in the West Lake, with 14 hectares areas and the green coverage rate reaches to 95 percent. On the east is the landscape of lakes and mountains. On the west is the Nanshan scenic spot. Several distinctive buildings are dotted in the mountains and rivers.

花家山庄是一家别墅式旅游度假饭店,周恩来总理也曾到访过。山庄地处西湖十里杨公堤南首,占地 14 公顷,绿化率 95％以上,东览湖光山色,西眺南山胜境,各具特色的建筑点缀在青山绿水之中。

2.4.5.6 Diaoyutai Hotel Hangzhou 杭州泛海钓鱼台酒店

The number of hotels that can be designated as hotels for LICs' reception is not large enough. Diaoyutai Hotel Hangzhou, opened in August 2016, has filled the vacancy. What's more, Diaoyutai Hotel Hangzhou features distinctive characteristics. Diaoyutai State Guesthouse in Beijing, the Chinese Foreign Ministry's venue for hosting heads of state, is inaugurated as an important venue for Chinese leaders conducting foreign affairs and state activities. Diaoyutai Hotel Hangzhou, a branch of Diaoyutai State Guesthouse, served several important guests from home and abroad during the Summit.

杭州可用于大规模的国际会议接待的酒店数量不够,泛海钓鱼台酒店作为 2016 年 8 月新开业的酒店,很好地弥补了这一空缺。并且,杭州泛海钓鱼台酒店有其自己的特色。钓鱼台国宾馆,是中国国家领导人进行外事活动的重要场所,更是国家接待各国元首和重要客人的超星级宾馆。而杭州泛海钓鱼台酒店是钓鱼台国宾馆的杭州分支,同样在这次 G20 峰会服务了不少国内外贵宾。

Figure 2-14　A Guestroom in Diaoyutai Hotel Hangzhou
图 2-14　杭州钓鱼台酒店客房一览

The hotel consists of 162 elegant guestrooms, 91 of which have a view of Qiantang River and some of which can enjoy a more magnificent view of the River from three different angles. Besides, suites with a 3.5-meter-long balcony, from which guests can enjoy the view of the river when both the tide is at its high and low, can give guests an unparalleled experience.

在酒店的 162 间客房中，91 间可以欣赏到钱塘江景，其中更有 270 度江景的豪华套房，让你的感官体验更加壮美开阔。此外，套房还拥有近 3.5 米宽的江景阳台，不论在平日欣赏平静宽阔的钱塘江带来的静谧平和，或是每年涨潮时观赏波涛汹涌的江面带来的意气风发，都是无与伦比的感受。

2.5 Foreign-related Etiquette Started with Me
涉外礼仪我先行

2.5.1 Brief Introduction 简介

For LICs, foreign-related etiquette can be used quite extensively. In general, it mainly focuses on the etiquette among LICs' representatives and staff of home and abroad. However, since a LIC usually brings a large number of foreign journalists and tourists to the host city, it is necessary for staff of service posts, cultural and sport workers, students and even each citizen to improve the sense of courtesy, to learn and adopt some foreign-related etiquette.

对于大型国际会议来说，涉外礼仪的使用范围非常广泛。一般来说，人们主要聚焦于参会的中外代表和工作人员之间的涉外礼仪。但是，由于大型国际会议会给一个城市带来大量的外国记者和游客，因此，整个城市的服务岗位人员、文体工作者、学生乃至每一位市民都有必要来提高礼貌意识，学习并应用涉外礼仪。

2.5.1.1 The difference between the bilateral and multilateral conferences
双边和多边会议的区别

LICs are usually multilateral conferences instead of bilateral ones. The higher profile the conferences have, the heavier responsibility the protocol departments own. For example, the Protocol Department of Ministry of Foreign Affairs of the People's Republic of China takes responsibility for the protocol affairs of such a high-profile conference like the G20 Hangzhou Summit.

大型国际会议往往是多边的。会议规格越高，会议的礼宾工作责任也就越重大。比如像 G20 杭州峰会这样知名度高的多边会议，礼宾这块会由中华人民共和国外交部礼宾司总体负责。

When it comes to the foreign affairs of a country, "No issues in diplomacy are small" should always be followed as one of the principles. "The details make the difference." For example, the fact that an authorized newspaper once mismatched a report of a foreign event with a wrong photo was tabooed in terms of foreign-related etiquette.

如果从外交的层面讲，"外事无小事"一定是必须奉行的其中一条原则。"细节决定成败"，之前就有国内权威报刊报道某外事活动出现图文不符的情况，这在涉外礼仪上就犯了禁忌。

The following parts will explain to the differences between bilateral conferences and multilateral ones from the perspectives of arrival and departure, greetings (including group photos), meetings, evening parties and banquets.

以下将从迎送抵离、会见(含合影)、会谈、晚会及宴请几个方面来谈谈双边和多边的礼仪差别。

In terms of arrival and departure, in the case of the political bilateral diplomatic conferences, normally the ministerial-level officials or above are recieved with the picking-up at the airport. The specific man for picking-up in the airport will be different depending on the guest country and the position of the guests. When it comes to a country's president or prime minister, a grand welcoming ceremony is usually set in the picking-up, which often consists of firing a salute and inspecting the three armed forces. On the other hand, in the case of multilateral diplomatic conferences, a clear difference during arrival and departure is that the host need take all the participating countries equal by assigning officials of same level (like ambassadors) for airport pick-up, normally without any specific welcoming ceremonies for any specific country. Regardless of political or non-political conferences, the protocol staff should take the initiative to shake hands with foreign guests and introduce on-spot officials (including name and position) to them. Due to cultural differences, some foreign guests tend to take the initiative to embrace to show their friendship. In that case, we must be courteous to offer a proper response. Flowers should be arranged after handshake.

在迎送抵离方面,若是政治性的双边外交会议,一般会安排部级及以上的干部前去接机,具体接机人员的设定视到访国家和到访人员的职级而定。若是一国总统或总理到访,常设隆重的欢迎仪式,仪式中常设有鸣礼炮或检阅三军等程序。但如果是多边外交会议,那么在迎送抵离环节中区别很明显的一点是必须平衡各个国家,安排同一级别的官员(比如大使)进行接机,一般没有特设的重大仪式。无论政治性还是非政治性会议,外宾下飞机(车)后,礼宾人员都应主动将迎宾人员(姓名和职务)介绍给外宾。迎宾人员随即与外宾握手表示欢迎。若因文化差异,部分外宾主动拥抱以示友好时,我方须有礼有节。献花须安排在握手欢迎之后。

In terms of greetings (including taking group photos), the host or the staff should wait for the guests in front of the main entrance of the building or the reception room. Except leaders' escort and interpreters, other persons should stay out of the leaders meeting to avoid mess. When guests leave, the host or the staff should stay at the main entrance of the building or the reception room to shake hands to bid farewell. The background and the standing position of guests are two key elements in a LIC group photo. Usually, the national flag of the host stands in the center of the background with the flags of other participants sequenced according to the alphabetical order (A, B, C...) of their names. The standing position of guests could be varying according to the specific situation. Generally speaking, the right side of the leader of the host country is more honorable.

在会见(含合影)方面,主人或主办方工作人员应在大楼正门或会客厅门口迎候。领导人会见中,除陪见人和译员外,其他陪同人员都应退出,避免场面混乱。送客时,可在大楼正门或会客厅门口握手送别。合影时,背景和合影站位是大型国际会议中非常关键的两个要素。背景的国旗通常以主办方为中心,按国家英文名称首字母排序,如 ABC 这一顺序。合影站位可视具体情况排列,一般来说主人右手边为上。

In terms of meetings, bilateral meetings are often provided with sofa set when there are only a few participants. An oval table is needed if there is further discussion. Even in a LIC, bilateral meetings are in the schedule. If two national flags are required to be hung in bilateral meetings, the flags of the two countries need to be placed at the same level. Taking the front face of the flags as the criterion, the international practice is to hang the flag of the visitor at the right side and to hang the flag of the host at the left side. On the other hand, a multilateral meeting with a round table is usually a worldwide practice, which normally considers a round table proper for multicultural cases. Therefore, many venues are designed to be in a round shape (such as the main stadium for the National Students' Sports Meeting in 2017). Above all, we could find that the positioning with foreign-related etiquette is usually following the principle that the right side is more honorable.

在会谈方面,双边会见在人员较少的情况下通常会安排沙发椅组就座,如有会谈,安排椭圆形桌。即便是在大型国际会议中,也会安排双边会谈。双边会谈中若须悬挂国旗,两国国旗要并挂,以旗身正面为准,国际惯例是右挂客方国旗,左挂本国国旗。而多边会见一般安排圆桌。在世界惯例中,圆桌会谈一般适合多边场合,所以许多场馆也设计成圆形(如 2017 年全国学生运动会的主体育场的圆形设计)。凡此种种,我们发现,涉外礼仪的许多排位均符合以右为上的原则。

In terms of evening parties and banquets, invitation letters must be placed in the guests' room or delivered to guests in advance. Seats should be set up according to international etiquette. Every procedure and link issues of the banquet need to be properly arranged. For example, the welcome banquet of the G20 Hangzhou Summit was held in Zhejiang Xizi Hotel. After the banquet, delegates moved to visit West Lake and finally watched the show "Most Memorable Is Hangzhou," which is held in the site of original "Impression on West Lake" show. Preparatory committee, Liaison officers and related staff had lots of consideration and rehearsals in order to control well the time and the transfer of all delegates.

在晚会及宴请方面,请柬须提前放置于宾客房间或交给宾客。晚会及宴请的席位或桌次应符合国际礼仪,流程和各种衔接事宜要安排妥当。如 G20 杭州峰会的欢迎晚宴安排在浙江西子宾馆,晚宴后从浙江西子宾馆移步游湖,最后至原"印象西湖"演出点附近观看"最忆是杭州"的演出。这个过程中时间的把控、人员的转移等问题都是筹备办、联络员及相关工作人员经过多方考虑和精心演练的。

2. 5. 1. 2 Elements and principles in foreign-related etiquette 涉外礼仪的要素和原则

Complete foreign-related etiquette consists of three different elements—good appearance, proper behavior and skillful communication. For example, subordinates should be introduced to superiors first. Polite expression is necessary in communication. Neither should we criticize peers or colleagues in the party or government nor try to spy on others' privacy. Euphemistic rejection is an art of communication that we should keep in mind.

完整的涉外礼仪包括三个要素——良好的外表形象、得体的行为举止和娴熟的交往技能。比如介绍的时候要符合尊者先知,即先把位低者介绍给位高者认识。交谈过程中注意礼貌用语,不能非议党政或同行同事,不要试图窥探对方的隐私,注意婉拒的艺术等。

We should follow some principles in foreign-related communication. For example, we should be neither humble nor pushy. Proper and thoughtful etiquette is indispensable but national dignity must be guarded. Never divulge a secret or do anything insulting motherland. Another example is the honesty principle, which guides us to attach great attention to any promise and agreement in LICs. Following the international practice is undoubtedly an emphasized principle. For example, some religious customs must be respected. We can't ask delegates from Muslim countries to remove their scarf while taking ID photo.

在涉外交往中,我们也必须遵循一些交往原则。比如不卑不亢的原则,既要以礼相待,又要维护本国尊严。礼节周到而得体适度,坚决不泄密,不做有辱我方的事情。再如诚信原则,大型国际会议中如若出现许诺、合约等应十分重视,尽量恪守。遵循国际惯例无疑是值得强调的一个原则。比如为穆斯林国家代表拍摄证件照时,不能要求对方摘下头巾,要尊重对方的宗教习俗。

2. 5. 2 Words, Phrases and Sentences 词汇、短语与例句

foreign-related etiquette 涉外礼仪

the sense of courtesy 礼貌意识

the Protocol Department 礼宾司

a high-profile conference 一场高规格会议

welcoming ceremony 欢迎仪式

fire a salute 鸣礼炮

take the initiative to shake hands 主动握手

introduce on-spot officials 介绍到场官员

international practice 国际惯例

euphemistic rejection 婉拒

be neither humble nor pushy 不卑不亢

national dignity 民族尊严

the honesty principle 诚信原则

religious customs 宗教习俗

（1）However, since a LIC usually brings a large number of foreign journalists and tourists to the host city, it is necessary for staff of service posts, cultural and sport workers, students and even each citizen to improve the sense of courtesy, to learn and adopt some foreign-related etiquette.

但是,由于大型国际会议会给一个城市带来大量的外国记者和游客,因此, 整个城市的服务岗位人员、文体工作者、学生乃至每一位市民都有必要来提高礼 貌意识,学习并应用涉外礼仪。

（2）When it comes to the foreign affairs of a country, "No issues in diplomacy are small" should always be followed as one of the principles.

如果从外交的层面讲,"外事无小事"一定是必须奉行的其中一条原则。

（3）Usually, the national flag of the host stands in the center of the background with the flags of other participants sequenced according to the alphabetical order (A, B, C...) of their names.

背景的国旗通常以主办方为中心,按国家英文名称首字母排序,如 ABC 这 一顺序。

（4）Complete foreign-related etiquette consists of three different elements—good appearance, proper behavior and skillful communication.

完整的涉外礼仪包括三个要素——良好的外表形象、得体的行为举止和娴 熟的交往技能。

2.5.3 Situational Practice 情景演练

You are assigned to work in the conference taskforce for a LIC on cross-border electronic business which involves totally more than 1,000 delegates and media staff from over 20 countries. You are in charge of contacting with a French delegation before they arrive in China as well as other airport and hotel issues. During the whole process, what are the points you need to pay attention to and how can you successfully fulfill this task?

你被分配到一个关于跨境电商的大型国际会议筹备组,这场会议总共有来自 20 多个国家的 1000 多名代表和媒体人员参加。你负责法国代表团的邮件联系、机场迎送和酒店安排事宜。在这整个过程中,你需要注意什么? 该如何成功地完成这项任务?

Suggested plan (Please feel free to complement where there is an ellipsis mark):

参考计划(请在标有省略号的地方自由补充你的想法):

(1)As to contacting work, e-mail is the best way to contact the French delegation because there is a large time gap and French usually prefer e-mails as a major cross-national communication method. While dealing with e-mails with French delegates, I should pay attention to the following points.

✓Engage in helping them settle down on reservations for airplanes and hotels...

✓If they've anything to consult about the schedule or other information on the conference, reply in time to let them get clear about these issues...

✓Make sure your e-mail is brief and to the point almost without grammatical or spelling mistakes...

(1) 关于联络方面的工作,由于时差很大,并且法国人偏爱将邮件往来作为跨国交流的主要方式,电子邮件是和法国代表团沟通的最佳方式。在和法国代表邮件往来的过程中,我要注意以下几点。

✓帮助他们一起来处理航班和酒店的预定问题。……

✓外宾咨询会议日程和其他信息时,及时回复以便让他们清楚这些事项。……

✓确保邮件简洁明了,尽量避免语法和拼写错误。……

(2)As to airport stuff, since I'm going to pick the delegation up and send them off, I do need to search about the route and arrange details such as buses and how to welcome them. In order to fulfill this part successfully, I ought to:

✓Do research about French customs to know how to get along well with them. For example, French people are... , but they don't like...

✓Pay attention to foreign-related etiquette during the welcoming and seeing-off period. Besides, it is quite crucial to take care of them or even their luggage on the way between airport and the hotel...

✓Make the right choice about the dress code. For example, males should wear suits while females ought to wear a businesslike suit (skirt or pants) or dress...

(2)关于机场的工作,既然我负责这些代表的迎接和送离,我需要调查清楚路线及接送的汽车和欢迎方式等其他细节。为了顺利完成这部分的工作,我应该:

✓研究并了解法国人的风俗习惯,以便和他们相处愉快。比如,法国人是……的,但是他们不喜欢……

✓在迎送期间注意涉外礼仪。除此之外,在机场和酒店的路上要注意照顾他们,包括帮他们一起照看行李。……

✓确保衣着得体。比如,男士建议穿西装,女士应该穿商务套装(裙子或裤子的套装皆可)或者商务连衣裙。……

(3)As to hotel stuff, since the French haven't been to the hotel before and this is the first stop right after the airport. In order to fulfill this part, I ought to:

✓Inform the hotel earlier about the delegation's arrival and departure if possible...

✓Make sure that you leave some time for the delegation to have a rest or some private time in their room after check-in. Do not arrange meals directly after they check in...

✓Act as a mediator in the hotel if it's necessary to help handle some problems such as luggage transportation, check-in and check-out issues; especially in terms of other special requirements put forward by the delegation since I know them better...

(3) 关于酒店的工作,由于法国人从未去过这个酒店,而酒店是他们下飞机后的第一站。为了顺利完成这部分的工作,我应该:

✓如果可能的话,早点通知酒店法国代表团的到达和离开时间。……

✓当代表办理完入住手续以后,确保留出一定的时间让他们休息或者自行安排。不要在办完入住手续以后直接安排就餐。……

✓如有需要,在酒店和代表之间充当一个协调人的角色。比如帮助处理行李运送、入住和离开等事宜,尤其是在代表提出一些特殊要求时,可以出来协调,因为我比酒店更了解他们。……

2.5.4 Extensive Links 拓展链接

Extensive links are set here to provide knowledge on some foreign rituals with the major countries who participate in LICs held in China frequently. Material collection together with bilingual interpretation of this book will help you to apply these languages and skills to the practical contacts with representatives from these countries.

拓展链接部分为大家提供的涉外礼仪知识主要针对的是频繁参与在华举办的大型国际会议的国家。资料整理加上本书的双语解读,有助于大家在和这些国家代表的实践交往中,真正运用这些语言和技能。

2.5.4.1 Euro-American countries 欧美国家

Don't speak to Europeans and Americans when your mouth are full of food and remember to cover your mouth with one hand when picking your teeth. As to gestures, thumb up means intending to take a ride in the United States and France. There are two meanings about stretching the forefinger and middle finger in the United Kingdom: Palms toward the other represent victory; if the back of the hand is toward other, it is a way of affront.

与欧美人谈话时不能满口食物,剔牙时要用一只手掩着口。手势方面,跷拇指在美国、法国表示拦路搭车。伸食指和中指在英国则有两种含义:手掌朝着对方,表示胜利;若手背朝着对方,则表示侮辱。

In the conversation, the two sides can not be too close and the voice can not be too high; do not rashly ask the ladies about age or marital status; it is better to speak frankly and righteously and do not whisper in front of the crowd; for religious beliefs and political insights, westerners are very serious, so do not rashly talk about this topic.

交谈过程中,双方不可靠得太近,谈话声音不可太高;不要轻率询问女士的年龄、婚姻状况;说话要光明正大,忌在大庭广众面前耳语;西方人对宗教信仰和政治见解很严肃,不能随意谈论。

2.5.4.2 Japan 日本

In Japan, when the business cards need to be exchanged, the low status side or the younger one should take the initiative to give cards to the other, meanwhile the business card should be pointed right at the other; in most occasion, the size of women's business card is smaller than men's. When you have a conversation with Japanese, do not gesticulate profusely or criticize indiscriminately and remember not to interrupt others' speech; if there are more than three persons in a conversation, do not neglect any people; do not use "old," "old man/woman" or other words to those aged men and women. The elder you talk with, the more taboos you need to be aware of.

在日本,交换名片时,地位低或年轻的一方应该先给对方,同时要将名片正对着对方;女性名片的尺寸大多比男性名片小。与日本人交谈时,不要边说边指手画脚,别人讲话时切忌插话打断;三人以上讲话时,注意不要冷落旁人;对年事高的男士和女士不要用"年迈""老人"等字样,面对年事越高的人越要注意忌讳。

2.5.4.3 South Korea 韩国

Traditional greeting etiquette of South Korea is bowing, which shall be 45 degrees. When people meet or separate, they should often use greetings and appreciation words. While calling others, South Koreans use honorifics and honorific titles in most occasions. Everyone is required to lower your head to say thanks, which is also a very important etiquette (The extent of lowering depends on a person's age and ranking relationship).

见面时,韩国传统礼节是鞠躬,而且要 45 度。相见或分手时要问候及致道谢辞。在称呼上多使用敬语和尊称。道谢时一定要低头致谢,这也是非常重要的礼节(低头的程度视对方的年龄、上下级关系而不同)。

2.5.4.4 Australia 澳大利亚

Australians like dressing casually and generally they won't wear a suit unless they attend a formal place. If you want to interact with a child, you must obtain the consent from his/her parents in advance. What's more, you should not touch the child's head or contact with his/her body, so as not to have the suspicion of harassment.

澳大利亚人衣着很随便,不出席正规场所一般不会穿西装。如果想和孩子互动,一定要事先征得家长的同意。切忌随意抚摸孩子的头或与其发生身体接触,以免有骚扰的嫌疑。

Regardless of social status and age, Australians like to have direct eye contact with people in conversation. At the same time, Australians would like to maintain a proper distance between each other. If it is not necessary, less than one meter away from someone will make them uncomfortable.

无论社会地位如何或处于哪个年龄阶段,澳大利亚人都喜欢在对话时与对方有直接的视线接触。同时,澳大利亚人喜欢保持适当的空间距离,如非必要,距离他人一米以内,会让其感到不舒服。

2.5.4.5 Russia 俄罗斯

The Orthodox is the main religion in Russia. Russians emphasize on cultural education, enjoy art and art appreciation. Russians don't have sea cucumber, jellyfish, cuttlefish or fungus. Their luck number is 7. In their opinion, "7" indicates success and can also bring happiness.

东正教是大多数俄罗斯人信奉的宗教。俄罗斯人重视文化教育,喜欢艺术品和艺术鉴赏;不吃海参、海蜇、墨鱼、菌类;偏爱 7,认为"7"象征成功,还可以给人们带来美满和幸福。

2.5.4.6 Brazil 巴西

Brazilians love to go straight, so they often speak out what is in their mind. Most Brazilians are lively, humorous, joke-liking in interpersonal relationships. At present, Brazilians in social occasions usually embrace or kiss as meeting etiquette. Only in very formal activities did they shake hands.

巴西人喜欢直来直去,有什么就说什么。巴西人在人际交往中大都活泼好动,幽默风趣,爱开玩笑。目前,巴西人在社交场合通常都以拥抱或者亲吻作为见面礼节。只有在十分正式的活动中,他们才相互握手为礼。

2.5.4.7 Argentina 阿根廷

Daily communication etiquette of Argentineans is roughly consistent with other European countries and it is influenced by the Spanish for the most. Most Argentineans are Catholic, so some religious rituals are often seen in the daily life.

阿根廷人在日常交往中所采用的礼仪与欧美其他国家大体上是一致的,受西班牙影响最深。阿根廷人大都信奉天主教,所以一些宗教礼仪也经常见诸阿根廷人的日常生活。

In communication, the handshake is generally adopted. In dealing with people they meet, Argentines believe that the more times you shake hands with each other, the better it is. In social situations, it is general to call the Argentineans "Sir" and "Miss" or "Mrs."

在交际中,普遍采取握手礼。在与交往对象相见时,阿根廷人认为与对方握手的次数多多益善。在交际场合,对阿根廷人一般均可以"先生""小姐"或"夫人"相称。

2.5.4.8 Mexico 墨西哥

Mexicans are easy to get along with because they are romantic, handsome and elegant. They like romantic and free life and are willing to live freely. Everyone likes cactus, as it's a national treasure. The taboos are yellow and red flowers.

墨西哥人好相处,潇洒大方有风度。生活浪漫喜自由,愿意无拘又无束。人人喜欢仙人掌,视为国宝倍爱护。忌讳黄色和红色的花。

Mexicans are generally not used to arriving on time in the appointment. They would always be late around 15 minutes to half an hour. However, they see it as a formality.

墨西哥人在赴约时,一般都不习惯准时到达,总愿迟到 15 分钟至半小时左右。他们把这样看成是一种礼节风度。

2.5.4.9 Indonesia 印度尼西亚

In Indonesia, when they visit relatives and friends, there are strict rules. Take off your shoes before entering the rooms and send the name card in the first meeting, otherwise, you will be ignored. If you pass something with your left hand, the other person will think that you do not respect him. If your right hand is occupied and have to use the left hand, you must say "sorry" to apologize. Indonesia people prefer jasmine.

探亲访友有讲究,未曾进屋鞋先脱,相识先要送名片,不然必会受冷落。如用左手递东西,对方会觉得不尊重他。如你实在腾不出右手而不得不用左手递时,一定要说声"对不起",以示歉意。印度尼西亚人偏爱茉莉花。

2.5.4.10 India 印度

While talking with Indians, do not involve their wives and children. They love to talk about their ancient cultural achievements and their cultural contributions to human civilization, as well as foreign events.

与印度人交谈时千万不要涉及他们的妻儿,他们喜欢谈论本国古老的文化成就及本国文化对人类文明的贡献,以及国外的事。

When it comes to answering questions, if your head tilts to one side or you shake heads, it is an affirmative answer. Do not misunderstand to cause unnecessary trouble.

回答对方问题时,如将头歪向一边或摇头,那是肯定的表示,千万别会错了意,造成不必要的麻烦。

2.5.4.11 Saudi Arabia 沙特阿拉伯

Mecca of Saudi, the birthplace of Islam, has a high reputation; so Saudi Arabian embrace religious canon strictly and pay attention to rituals and taboo; in their view, left hand is not clean, and photography cannot be done freely; generally the nation is upright, warm and generous and etiquette-oriented.

沙特麦加有声誉,伊斯兰教发祥地;宗教信仰教规严,注重祭典和禁忌;左手认为不干净,照相千万别随意;国民一般很耿直,大方热情重礼仪。

Saudi Arabia is populated with Muslim mostly, but there are a small amount of Christians. Politics in the Middle East and international oil should be avoided in the conversation.

沙特阿拉伯人大多信奉伊斯兰教,还有少数人信奉基督教。交谈时应回避中东政治问题和国际石油问题。

2.5.4.12 South Africa 南非

Social etiquette of South African can be summarized as "totally different between the white and the dark" and "mainly British style." "Totally different between the white and the dark" refers to the fact that social etiquettes of South

Africa's white group are absolutely different from the dark one since they are restricted by race, religion and customs; "mainly British style" is because during a long historical period in South Africa, the white group mastered the regime. So social etiquette of the white, especially British style, prevails in South African society.

南非社交礼仪可以概括为"黑白分明"和"英式为主"。"黑白分明"是指受到种族、宗教、习俗的制约,南非的黑人和白人的社交礼仪不同;"英式为主"是指在很长的一段历史时期内,白人掌握南非政权,白人的社交礼仪特别是英国式社交礼仪盛行于南非社会。

2.5.4.13 Turkey 土耳其

Turks believe in Islam. They like to drink alcohol other than wine and they like to eat beef, mutton while pork is forbid. Turks prefer patterns of pigs, cats and pandas.

土耳其人信仰伊斯兰教,他们喜欢喝葡萄酒以外的酒,喜欢吃牛肉、羊肉,忌吃猪肉,喜欢猪、猫、熊猫的图案。

Since it is not easy to remember the names of some Turks, it is better to bring enough name cards to exchange with the Turks. After receiving the name cards, try to pronounce the name correctly, and if necessary, ask someone else to correct it.

由于有些土耳其人的姓名不太容易记,最好带上足够的名片,同遇到的土耳其人互相交换。接到名片后,要试着把上面的名字念准,请别人替自己纠正。

Chapter 3

Hangzhou Welcomes You: Bilingual Information of Tours

杭州欢迎您:资讯出行双语通

3.1 General Information of Basic Needs
衣食住行资讯概况

3.1.1 Hangzhou 杭州

Situated to the south of the Yangtze River Delta, Hangzhou is the capital of Zhejiang Province in East China. Incorporated as a city 2,200 years ago, its history even dates back to local Liangzhu Culture (3400—2250 BC) of Neolithic settlements. Adored as paradise on the Earth, Hangzhou is China's leading cultural and scenic destination that blends profound heritage with breathtaking river, lake and mountain views. Among Hangzhou's numerous attractions, the West Lake and the Grand Canal, two world heritage sites, are both historic and scenic marvels adjoining and within the city. Hangzhou, celebrated as China's culinary mecca, also takes pride in offering visitors an exciting range of local, national and international delights.

杭州位于长江三角洲的南部,是中国东部省份浙江的省会城市。杭州建市已有2200余年,其历史甚至可以追溯到新石器时代的良渚文化时期(前3400—前2250)。被誉为"人间天堂"的杭州是中国首屈一指的文化和风景名胜地,拥有瑰丽的自然和文化遗产,风光旖旎的河流、湖泊、山川。在杭州的众多景点中,西湖和京杭大运河这两个拥有大美景色和丰富历史文化底蕴的世界文化遗产交相辉映。杭州,被誉为中国的美食圣地,致力于为各方游客提供各式各样的美食,包括当地美食、中国美食及国际美食。

3.1.2 Climate 气候

Hangzhou has a climate of subtropical monsoon type with four quite distinct seasons as spring, summer, autumn and winter. The G20 Hangzhou Summit was held in September. September in Hangzhou is characterized by sunny, crisp days. Afternoon showers are possible, making it cool and cozy in the evening. The average lowest and highest temperatures are 20°C (68°F) and 28°C (82°F) respectively. Please be advised to bring summer clothes.

杭州属亚热带季风性气候,有春夏秋冬四个截然不同的季节。G20 峰会于 9 月份召开。杭州的 9 月以晴朗干爽的天气居多。人们可以在午后冲凉以在晚上保持凉爽舒适。杭州 9 月的平均最低温和最高温分别是 20°C (68°F) 和 28°C (82°F)。建议您准备好夏装。

3.1.3 Time Zone 时区

Hangzhou subjects to Beijing Standard Time, which is 8 hours ahead of GMT. DST is not adopted in China.

杭州以北京时间为准,比格林尼治时间早八个小时。中国不采用夏令时。

3.1.4 Currency and ATM Service 货币和自助取款服务

The official currency of China is RMB. Retailers in Hangzhou generally do not accept other currencies so it is necessary for visitors to change foreign currency into RMB in advance in order to make cash payments. No restrictions are imposed on the amount of foreign currencies, traveler's checks or credit cards to be brought into China. However, non-residents carrying more than USD 5,000 (or equivalent in other foreign currencies) or RMB 20,000 in cash should declare to the Customs. Major world currencies and travelers' checks can be converted to/from RMB. Currency exchange points are located at Hangzhou Xiaoshan International Airport, main hotels and banks throughout the city. Banks usually take commission for money exchange and participants are advised to take it into consideration. When making a currency exchange, some banks also require a passport or other documents. Automated Teller Machines (ATMs) are found throughout the city. It is also possible to use the ATMs located in banks, hotels and large shopping centers.

中国的官方货币是人民币。杭州的商户一般不接受其他货币,因此游客需提前将外币兑换成人民币,以便用现金支付。对于进入中国的外币、旅行支票或信用卡的金额不做限制。但是,非中国居民携带超过 5000 美元(或等值的其他外币)或人民币 20000 元现金入境时应向海关申报。主要世界货币和旅行支票都可以兑换成人民币。货币兑换点位于杭州萧山国际机场及遍布整座城市主要酒店和银行。银行通常收取货币兑换佣金,望兑换者悉知。在进行货币兑换时,一些银行还需要护照或其他文件。自动取款机(ATM)遍布整个城市,也可以使用位于银行、酒店和大型购物中心的自动取款机。

3.1.5 Credit Cards 信用卡

Visa, MasterCard, American Express, JCB, Diners Club and other major international credit cards are accepted at most establishments or can be used to get cash from ATMs throughout the city, although some small shops and restaurants may only accept cash payments.

Visa、MasterCard、美国运通、JCB、大来俱乐部和其他主要的国际信用卡可以在大多数机构使用,亦可用于从遍布整座城市的自动取款机提现。然而一些小商店和餐馆可能只接受现金付款。

3.1.6 Electricity and Water Supply 水电供应

The power supply in China is 220—240 volts, 50 hertz. Two/three-pronged plugs are used. Please check before using an appliance. Tap water is not drinkable directly. We advise the delegates to consume bottled water which can be purchased at the hotel or any nearby convenient stores.

中国的电源是 220—240 伏,50 赫兹。使用两孔/三孔插头。请在使用设备前检查。自来水不可直接饮用。我们建议代表在酒店或酒店附近的便利店购买瓶装水。

Figure 3-1　Jack-and-Plug in China

图 3-1　中国的插座和插头

3.1.7 Postal Service 邮政服务

Postal Service Post Offices generally open from 09:00 to 17:00.

邮局营业时间为 09:00—17:00。

3.1.8 Restaurants Information 餐厅信息

Information about local restaurants will be available at the LIC Information Desks.

当地餐厅的相关信息可向该大型国际会议的服务台获取。

3.1.9 Delegate Handbook 代表手册

All delegates will be provided with a Delegate Handbook upon accreditation.

所有认证代表都将得到一份代表手册。

3.1.10 Tipping 小费

Tipping is not customary for restaurant waiters or taxi drivers in China.

中国没有给餐厅服务员或出租车司机小费的传统。

3.1.11 Useful Telephone Numbers 常用号码

Police: 110; Fire: 119; and Medical: 120

报警电话:110;火警:119;急救:120

3. 1. 12 Mobile Phone Information 移动电话服务

Local phone services are reliable. Both GSM and CDMA mobile phone systems are in operation. Most modern cell phones can work in several settings that can use roaming service in different networks. Most of the GSM-phones in use in China support the protocols of GSM-900 and GSM-1800. Long distance calls within China may be made by direct dialing through International Direct Dial (IDD) in major cities or through operated assisted calls. Telex and Fax services are readily available in major hotels.

本地电话服务安全可靠。GSM 和 CDMA 移动电话系统都可使用。大多数手机经过设置之后都可以在不同网络中使用漫游服务。在中国使用的大多 GSM 电话支持 GSM-900 和 GSM-1800 协议。在中国境内的长途电话可以通过在主要城市直接拨打国际直拨电话(IDD)或通过操作辅助呼叫。主要酒店都可以使用电传和传真服务。

3. 1. 13 Smoking 关于吸烟

In Hangzhou, smoking is banned in all indoor public spaces and is also prohibited in open-air space in kindergartens, schools, child welfare institutions, women and children's hospitals, fitness and sports venues, and cultural relic sites that are open to the public, though designated areas are usually provided for smokers.

杭州所有的室内公共场所都是禁烟的,且幼儿园、学校、儿童福利院、妇幼保健院、健身场所、文物古迹等场所内的室外空间也是禁烟的,但通常会为吸烟者提供特定的吸烟区域。

3. 2 Tickets and Transportation
门票与交通

3. 2. 1 Tickets of Hangzhou International Expo Centre (HIEC)
杭州国际博览中心门票

Hangzhou International Expo Centre (HIEC), as the main venue of the G20 Hangzhou Summit, located in the Olympic Expo Centre in Hangzhou, will keep to be used to hold LICs in the future. On September 5, 2016, after the Summit closed, a lot of people were asking, "When will HIEC be open for public visit?" As expected, it has been open to the public since September 25, 2016 and the specific open hour is from 9:00 to 16:00. At present, it has mainly opened three regions: the reception area, the main venue and the luncheon area.

杭州国际博览中心是 G20 杭州峰会的主会场,位于杭州奥体博览城,今后也将用来承办大型国际会议。2016 年 9 月 5 日峰会结束后,就有很多人在问,何时能开放参观? 国博中心于 2016 年 9 月 25 日开始试开放,具体开放时间为 9:00—16:00。目前主要开放的是三个区域:迎宾区、主会场和午宴区。

Figure 3-2　Hangzhou International Expo Centre (HIEC)
图 3-2　杭州国际博览中心

➤ Address: 353 Benjing Avenue, Qianjiang Century City, Xiaoshan District, Hangzhou, Zhejiang Province

地址:浙江省杭州市萧山区钱江世纪城奔竞大道 353 号

➤Ticket price: RMB 150 per person for individual tourist; RMB 120 per person for the online purchasing; RMB 100 per person for group tourists. Individual and group tickets can be purchased on the spot; online tickets can be purchased at the related network termination by the venue's operating company.

参观票价:散客每人 150 元,网购价每人 120 元,团体票每人 100 元。散客票和团体票采取现场购买形式,网络票通过场馆运营公司相关网络端发售。

➤HIEC official website: http://www.hiechangzhou.com

杭州国际博览中心官网:http://www.hiechangzhou.com

3. 2. 2 Tickets of the "Impression of West Lake" Show
"印象西湖"演出门票

"Impression on West Lake" performance series currently include two shows: the original "Impression of West Lake" and "The Most Memorable Is Hangzhou." Both have been translated into one unified "Impression of West Lake" in the report by CCTV as well as foreign media. Actually "The Most Memorable is Hangzhou" is adapted from the original "Impression of West Lake." As the most impressive performance during the Leaders' Summit in Hangzhou, when the ordinary citizens watched it live on TV, it had caught our heart and triggered our desire to watch it on the spot. Fortunately, it had been open to the public finally from October 1 to November 10 in 2016! In the future, the show arrangement will be released on several ticket websites authorized by "Impression of West Lake" official website, for example, http://www.yxwestlake.com.

"印象西湖"演出系列目前包括原"印象西湖"和"最忆是杭州"两个系列。两者在央视和外媒报道中均统一翻译为"印象西湖"。"最忆是杭州"改编自"印象西湖",是杭州领导人峰会期间最为惊艳的演出。普通观众通过电视屏幕一睹"最忆是杭州"的风采之后,便魂牵梦萦,想要一睹真容。值得庆幸的是,它终于在 2016 年 10 月 1 日—11 月 10 日正式对民众公开售票演出啦! 后期的演出安排可关注印象西湖官网授权的一些售票网站,如 http://www.yxwestlake.com/。

➤Performance address: 22 Beishan Road, opposite of the Yue Temple, West Lake District, Hangzhou, Zhejiang Province

演出地点:浙江省杭州市西湖区北山路 22 号岳庙对面

➤Performance information: twice every day from 1 to 7 October, 2016, 50 minutes each session, the first session at 19:30—20:20, the second session 21:00—21:50, the majority of programs kept. From October 8 to November 10 in 2016, only one session at 19:30—20:20. Considering the large number of actors and the long-term operation, there will be some adjustments to the programs.

演出信息:2016 年 10 月 1 日—7 日每天两场,每场 50 分钟,第一场19:30—20:20,第二场 21:00—21:50,基本保留多数节目;10 月 8 日之后暂定只演19:30—20:20 的那一场。因演员较多,从长期运作考虑,节目会做一些调整。

➤Ticket Strategy 购票攻略:

Zone (Capacity)	Duration	Regular Rate	Special Rate with a citizen card
Grandstand (809)	Oct 1—Oct 7	¥350	¥210 (40% off)
	After Oct 7	¥300	¥180 (40% off)
VIP (324)	Oct 1—Oct 7	¥500	¥300 (40% off)
	After Oct 7	¥460	¥270 (40% off)
Presidential A (48)	Oct 1—Oct 7	¥1000	¥700 (30% off)
	After Oct 7	¥800	¥560 (30% off)
Presidential B (15)	Oct 1—Oct 7	¥1500	¥1050 (30% off)
	After Oct 7	¥1200	¥840 (30% off)
Presidential C (4)	Oct 1—Oct 7	¥2000	
	After Oct 7	¥1800	

Figure 3-3   Opening Time of "The Most Memorable Is Hangzhou" in 2016

座位区 (座位数)	时间段	门市票价	市民优惠价
主观众席(809)	10 月 1 日—10 月 7 日	¥350	¥210 (6 折)
	10 月 7 日以后	¥300	¥180 (6 折)
VIP (324)	10 月 1 日—10 月 7 日	¥500	¥300 (6 折)
	10 月 7 日以后	¥460	¥270 (6 折)
总统席 A 区 (48)	10 月 1 日—10 月 7 日	¥1000	¥700 (7 折)
	10 月 7 日以后	¥800	¥560 (7 折)
总统席 B 区(15)	10 月 1 日—10 月 7 日	¥1500	¥1050 (7 折)
	10 月 7 日以后	¥1200	¥840 (7 折)
总统席 C 区(4)	10 月 1 日—10 月 7 日	¥2000	
	10 月 7 日以后	¥1800	

图 3-3   2016 年"最忆是杭州"开放时间

(1) Hangzhou citizens enjoy discount tickets by presenting their own ID card with one ticket per person per day and enter the show by checking the ID card or the ticket;

(2) Children under 1.3 meters go to half-priced tickets while people above 1.3 meters purchase adult tickets;

(3) On-spot sale time is from 9:00 to 17:00 every day.

(1) 杭州市民均可凭本人身份证享受市民优惠折扣购票,每人每天限购 1 张,凭身份证及门票验证检票入场;

(2) 1.3 米以下的儿童半票,1.3 米以上的需购成人票;

(3) 现场售票时间为每天 9:00—17:00。

3.2.3 Traffic around Olympic Expo Centre
奥体博览城及杭州交通概况

Olympic Expo Centre, the centre of the road circle around Hangzhou, is located in the south riverside of Qiantang River, that is, the opposite of Qianjiang New CBD in Hangzhou with the river between each other. It's adjacent to Xiaoshan International Airport, Hangzhou-Ningbo expressway, Hangzhou-Jinhua-Quzhou expressway, Zhejiang-Jiangxi railway and Xiaoshan-Ningbo railway, which makes it geographically superior with very convenient traffic.

奥体博览城地处钱塘江南岸,杭州绕城公路圈中心,与杭州钱江新城隔江相望。毗邻杭州萧山国际机场、杭甬高速公路、杭金衢高速公路、浙赣及萧甬铁路,地理位置优越,道路交通便利。

Hangzhou has the common bus line and BRT line. The majority of metro line 1, 2 and 4 has been open; Line 1 to 10 will all be open before the opening of Asian Games in 2022.

杭州设有普通公交和快速公交线。杭州地铁 1 号、2 号和 4 号线目前已大部分开通,1 号线到 10 号线将于 2022 年亚运会举办之前全部开通。

Hangzhou Tourism Committee has set up quite a lot sightseeing advisory stations in Hangzhou City and its every district or county with free maps within the station. During the Summit, the bilingual audio maps were also published to provide more convenience for foreign visitors.

杭州市旅游委员会在杭州和杭州各个区、县、市设立了多个旅游咨询站,站内放有免费地图。峰会筹备期间还出版了双语有声版地图,为来杭外宾提供便利。

3.3 Culinary Recommendation
菜品推荐

The G20 welcome dinner, themed as "West Lake Feast," was held in Zhejiang Xizi Hotel. From the clothing of waiters to the tableware and the table, they all embodied the West Lake elements. Now let's introduce and recommend some famous Hangzhou dishes, which are not only constrained by state-level hotel for leaders' reception, but can also be tasted in more reasonably priced restaurants like Louwailou or other authentic local restaurant. These dishes are as follows:

G20 杭州峰会欢迎晚宴设于浙江西子宾馆，晚宴以"西湖盛宴"为主题。从服务员服装到餐具再到台面，无不透露着西湖元素。下面我们就来推介一些著名杭帮菜品。这些菜品不一定要在接待元首级别的国宾馆才能品尝到，在价格更为亲民的楼外楼或者其他正宗杭帮菜馆都能吃到。这些菜品有：

West Lake Fish in Vinegar Gravy 西湖醋鱼

Sweet and Sour Spare Ribs 糖醋排骨

Soy-sauced Dongpo Pork 东坡肉

Stewed Fish Head with Tofu in Pottery Pot 砂锅鱼头豆腐

Poached Chicken 白切鸡

Braised Duck with Soy Sauce 杭州卤鸭

Marinated Shrimp with Yellow Wine 杭州醉虾

Honey Lotus Root Stuffed with Glutinous Rice 桂花糯米藕

Sauteed Bamboo Shoot 油焖笋

Shredded Perch Soup with Ham and Ginger 宋嫂鱼羹

Shredded Pork Soup with Hot Pickled Mustard Tuber 榨菜肉丝汤

Stewed Spicy Mapo Tofu 麻婆豆腐

Braised Pork Ball in Brown Sauce 红烧狮子头

Omelet with Shredded Pork 木须肉

Wine Preserved Crab 醉蟹

Spring Chicken 童子鸡

Shredded Pork with Garlic Sauce 鱼香肉丝

Braised Pork Balls in Gravy Sauce 四喜丸子

Steamed Beef Ribs in Bean Sauce 豉汁牛仔骨

Moreover, during the Summit, the catering personnel around Hangzhou had demonstrated well the spiritual outlook of China. For example, through a year of training, the staff in Zhejiang Xizi Hotel acted in perfect unison while opening the bowl cover of the dish, serving a new dish, changing the towels and taking away the finished dish during the welcome dinner, which won appreciation from Chinese and foreign guests.

值得一提的是,在峰会期间,杭城各地餐饮服务人员很好地体现了中国的精神风貌。比如浙江西子宾馆工作人员经过一年的训练,在晚宴现场表现出来的齐刷刷地揭盖、上菜、换毛巾和撤菜等,赢得了中外来宾的赞赏。

3.4 Public Services and Health
公共服务与医疗

Hangzhou provides public bicycle rental services with free rent within one hour. Since October, 2002, West Lake has become the first and the only 5A scenic spot without any ticket fee and its lake parks are open 24 hours a day. Hangzhou Bus Group has launched two free networking projects in bus stops— "i-hangzhou" and "Gongjiao_free." When people are waiting for the bus at the bus station, as long as they use mobile terminals with WiFi function (mobile phones, laptops, tablets, etc.), the WiFi can be used in stations with the label "Free WiFi."

杭州提供公共自行车的租赁服务,一小时内免费租用。2002 年 10 月起,西湖成为全国第一个也是唯一一个不收门票的 5A 级景区,24 小时免费开放环湖公园。杭州公交集团推出公交站台免费联网"i-hangzhou"和"Gongjiao_free"两个项目。市民在公交车站等车时,只要使用带有 WiFi 功能的移动终端(手机、笔记本、平板电脑等),就可在标有"本站点可免费无线上网"这种醒目标签的站点使用网络。

Though there are medical clinics at meeting venues during meeting hours and at designated hotels round-the-clock, when it comes to chronic conditions, designated professional hospitals are needed to be available. The following listed are the addresses, contact info and official websites of designated hospitals in Hangzhou.

虽然在大型国际会议的会场开放时间和酒店运营的全天候时间里都设有医疗点,但若出现慢性症状,需要转到指定的专业医院。以下整理的是杭州指定医院的地址、联系方式和官网。

➢Zhejiang Hospital, 12 Lingyin Road, Hangzhou, Zhejiang Province, China. Tel:＋86-571-86999551. http://english.zjhospital.com.cn

浙江医院,中国浙江省杭州市灵隐路 12 号;联系电话:＋86-571-86999551;官网:http://zjhospital.com.cn

➤The First Affiliated Hospital, Zhejiang University School of Medicine 79 Qingchun Road, Hangzhou, Zhejiang Province, China. Tel：＋86-571-87231500. http://www.zy91.com

浙江大学附属第一医院,中国浙江省杭州市庆春路 79 号;联系电话:＋86-571-87231500;官网:http://www.zy91.com

➤ The Second Affiliated Hospital, Zhejiang University School of Medicine 88 Jiefang Road, Hangzhou, Zhejiang Province, China Tel：＋86-571-87315018. http://en.z2hospital.com

浙江大学附属第二医院,中国浙江省杭州市解放路 88 号;联系电话:＋86-571-87315018;官网:http://en.z2hospital.com

➤Sir Run Run Shaw Hospital Affiliated to School of Medcine, Zhejiang University 3 East Qingchun Road, Hangzhou, Zhejiang Province, China. Tel：＋86-571-86683088 http://www.srrsh-english.com

浙江大学邵逸夫附属医院,中国浙江省杭州市庆春东路 3 号;联系电话:＋86-571-86683088;官网:http://www.srrsh-english.com

Appendix | 附录

Appendix. 1 G20 Summit Opening Speech by President Xi Jinping
G20 峰会开幕式习近平总书记致辞

Dear Colleagues,

尊敬的各位同事：

Now, I declare that the G20 Hangzhou Summit begins.

我现在宣布，二十国集团领导人杭州峰会开幕！

It gives me great pleasure to meet you here in Hangzhou, and first of all, I wish to extend a very warm welcome to all of you.

很高兴同大家相聚杭州。首先，我谨对各位同事的到来，表示热烈欢迎！

Leaders' Group Photo Spot of the G20 Hangzhou Summit
G20 峰会主场馆领导人合影点

The G20 Summit in Antalya last year was a big success. And I wish to take this opportunity to thank Turkey once again for its outstanding job and the positive outcomes achieved during its presidency. Under the theme "Collective Action for Inclusive and Robust Growth," Turkey brought about progress in inclusiveness, implementation and investment. China highly commends Turkey's efforts on various fronts during its G20 presidency.

去年，二十国集团领导人安塔利亚峰会开得很成功。我也愿借此机会，再次感谢去年主席国土耳其的出色工作和取得的积极成果。土方以"共同行动以实现包容和稳健增长"作为峰会主题,从"包容、落实、投资"三方面推动产生成果,中方一直积极评价土方在担任主席国期间开展的各项工作。

In the next two days, under the theme of this Summit, we will have discussions on strengthening policy coordination, breaking a new path of growth, more effective and efficient global economic and financial governance, robust international trade and investment, inclusive and interconnected development as well as other issues affecting the world economy.

未来两天,我们将围绕杭州峰会主题,就加强宏观政策协调、创新增长方式,更高效的全球经济金融治理,强劲的国际贸易和投资,包容和联动式发展,影响世界经济的其他突出问题等议题展开讨论。

Eight years ago, at the height of the international financial crisis, the G20 acted in a spirit of unity and partnership, pulled the world economy back from the precipice and pushed it onto the track of stability and recovery. Today, eight years on, the global economy has again reached a critical juncture. The growth momentum generated by the last round of scientific and technological progress is diminishing, while the new round of scientific and industrial revolution has just started. Population aging is happening in all major economies and the decline in population growth puts economic and social pressure on countries. Economic globalization is suffering setbacks, protectionism and inward-looking trends are on the rise, and the multi-national trading regime is under pressure. Despite notable progress made in financial regulatory reform, the risks of excessive leverage and bubbles continue to build up. Under the impact of all these factors, the global economy, while still on the road to recovery, faces multiple risks and challenges such as weak growth momentum, sluggish demand, volatility in financial market and slow growth in international trade and investment.

8年前,在国际金融危机最紧要关头,二十国集团临危受命,秉持同舟共济的伙伴精神,把正在滑向悬崖的世界经济拉回到稳定和复苏轨道。8年后的今天,世界经济又走到一个关键当口。上一轮科技进步带来的增长动能逐渐衰减,新一轮科技和产业革命尚未形成势头。主要经济体先后进入老龄化社会,人口增长率下降,给各国经济、社会带来压力。经济全球化出现波折,保护主义、内顾倾向抬头,多边贸易体制受到冲击。金融监管改革虽有明显进展,但高杠杆、高泡沫等风险仍在积聚。在这些因素综合作用下,世界经济虽然总体保持复苏态势,但面临增长动力不足、需求不振、金融市场反复动荡、国际贸易和投资持续低迷等多重风险和挑战。

The G20 consists of the world's major economies. The international community has great expectations for the G20 and places high hopes on this Hangzhou Summit. I hope the Hangzhou Summit will provide a solution that addresses both the symptoms and root causes of the global economic problems and achieve strong, sustainable, balanced and inclusive global growth.

二十国集团聚集了世界主要经济体,国际社会对我们充满期待,对这次峰会寄予厚望。希望杭州峰会能够为世界经济开出一剂标本兼治、综合施策的"药方",让世界经济走上强劲、可持续、平衡、包容增长之路。

First, in the face of these challenges, we should strengthen macroeconomic policy coordination, and jointly promote global growth and uphold international financial stability. The G20 members should pursue more comprehensive macroeconomic policies in keeping with their own national realities, and coordinate their fiscal, monetary and structural reform policies in order to expand aggregate global demand, improve the quality of supply and bolster the foundation of growth. We should continue to strengthen policy coordination and reduce negative spillovers.

第一,面对当前挑战,我们应该加强宏观经济政策协调,合力促进全球经济增长、维护金融稳定。二十国集团成员应该结合本国实际,采取更加全面的宏观经济政策,统筹兼顾财政、货币、结构性改革政策,努力扩大全球总需求,全面改善供给质量,巩固经济增长基础。应该继续加强政策协调,减少负面外溢效应。

Second, in the face of these challenges, we should break a new path for growth and generate new growth momentum. The G20 should change its policy approach and place equal importance on both short-term and mid-to-long-term policies, and both demand-side management and supply-side reform. This year, we've agreed on the G20 Blueprint on Innovative Growth, and we've made the unanimous decision to break a new path and expand new frontier for world economy through innovation, structural reform, new industrial revolution and the development of the digital economy.

第二,面对当前挑战,我们应该创新发展方式,挖掘增长动能。二十国集团应该调整政策思路,做到短期政策和中长期政策并重,需求侧管理和供给侧改革并重。今年,我们已经就《二十国集团创新增长蓝图》达成共识,一致决定通过创新、结构性改革、新工业革命、数字经济等新方式,为世界经济开辟新道路,拓展新边界。

Third, in the face of these challenges, we should improve global economic governance, and strengthen institutional safeguards. The G20 should continue to improve the international monetary and financial system and the governance structure of international financial institutions, and fully leverage the role of the IMF's Special Drawing Rights. We should strengthen the global financial safety net and enhance cooperation in financial regulation, international taxation and combating corruption to boost the resilience of the world economy against risks. This year, we have restarted the G20 International Financial Architecture Working Group. I hope the Working Group will continue its work and become more effective.

第三,面对当前挑战,我们应该完善全球经济治理,夯实机制保障。二十国集团应该不断完善国际货币金融体系,优化国际金融机构治理结构,充分发挥国际货币基金组织特别提款权作用。应该完善全球金融安全网,加强在金融监管、国际税收、反腐败领域合作,提高世界经济抗风险能力。今年,我们重启了二十国集团国际金融架构工作组,希望继续向前推进,不断提高有效性。

Fourth, in the face of these challenges, we should build an open global economy, and continue to promote facilitation and liberalization of trade and investment. The G20 should honor its commitment of not adopting new protectionism measures, strengthen coordination and cooperation on investment policies, take credible steps to stimulate trade growth. Infrastructure connectivity should be enhanced so as to bring developing countries and small- and medium-sized companies into the global value chain, and make the global economy more open and integrated.

第四,面对当前挑战,我们应该建设开放型世界经济,继续推动贸易和投资自由化、便利化。二十国集团应该恪守不采取新的保护主义措施的承诺,加强投资政策协调合作,采取切实行动促进贸易增长。我们应该发挥基础设施互联互通的辐射效应和带动作用,帮助发展中国家和中小企业深入参与全球价值链,推动全球经济进一步开放、交流、融合。

Fifth, in the face of these changes, we should implement the 2030 Agenda for Sustainable Development and promote inclusive development. According to relevant statistics, the Gini coefficient has exceeded the widely-recognized alarm level of 0. 6, and reached around 0. 7 globally. This is something that we must pay close attention to. This year, development is high on the G20 agenda, and we have formulated an action plan to implement the 2030 Agenda for Sustainable Development. We'll also support industrialization in Africa and the least developed countries (LCD), expand energy access, promote financial inclusion, and encourage the young people to start their own businesses. Through these means and more, we can reduce the inequality and imbalance of global development, and deliver the benefits of global growth to people of all countries.

第五,面对当前挑战,我们应该落实 2030 年可持续发展议程,促进包容性发展。据有关统计,现在世界基尼系数已经达到 0. 7 左右,超过了公认的 0. 6 危险线,必须引起我们的高度关注。今年,我们把发展置于二十国集团议程的突出位置,共同制定落实 2030 年可持续发展议程行动计划。同时,我们还将通过支持非洲和最不发达国家工业化、提高能源可及性、发展普惠金融、鼓励青年创业等方式,减少全球发展不平等和不平衡,使各国人民共享世界经济增长成果。

Dear colleagues! The G20 carries high expectations of the international community. We must ensure that the G20 fully plays its role of keeping the world economy on the track of prosperity and stability.

尊敬的各位同事! 二十国集团承载着世界各国的期待,我们要努力把它建设好,为世界经济繁荣稳定把握好大方向。

First, the G20 must keep up with the changing times and lead the way forward. The G20 should adapt itself to the needs of the global economy, and further transform itself from a mechanism of crisis response to one of long-term governance. When major issues emerge, the G20 has the responsibility to play a leading role, and with a strategic vision, set the direction and blaze the trail for global growth.

第一,与时俱进,发挥引领作用。二十国集团应该根据世界经济需要,进一步从危机应对向长效治理机制转型。面对重大突出问题,二十国集团有责任发挥领导作用,展现战略视野,为世界经济指明方向,开拓路径。

Second, the G20 should fully honor its commitment. We should make the G20 an action team instead of a talk shop. This year, we have formulated action plans for many areas, such as sustainable development, green finance, energy efficiency, and combatting corruption. And each and every plan should be implemented.

第二,知行合一,采取务实行动。我们应该让二十国集团成为行动队,而不是清谈馆。今年,我们在可持续发展、绿色金融、提高能效、反腐败等诸多领域制定了行动计划,要把每一项行动落到实处。

Third, the G20 should become a platform of cooperation built through joint efforts that deliver benefits to all. We should continue to strengthen the institutional building of the G20 to sustain and deepen our cooperation. We should solicit proposals for improvement and heed the views of all countries especially the developing countries so as to make the G20 more inclusive and better respond to the demands of people of different countries.

第三,共建共享,打造合作平台。我们应该继续加强二十国集团机制建设,确保合作延续和深入。广纳良言,充分倾听世界各国特别是发展中国家的声音,使二十国集团工作更具包容性,更好地回应各国人民的诉求。

Fourth, the G20 should stick together as partners in confronting challenges. The G20 countries differ in national conditions, stages of development, and face different challenges, but we all share a common goal of pursuing stronger growth, meeting challenges and achieving common development. So long as we stick together, we can navigate the heavy waves of the global economy and sail towards a future of growth.

第四,同舟共济,发扬伙伴精神。我们虽然国情不同、发展阶段不同、面临的现实挑战不同,但推动经济增长的愿望相同,应对危机挑战的利益相同,实现共同发展的憧憬相同。只要我们坚持同舟共济的伙伴精神,就能够克服世界经济的惊涛骇浪,开辟未来增长的崭新航程。

Dear colleagues! In preparing for this Hangzhou Summit, China has followed the principle of openness, transparency and inclusiveness, and we have maintained close contact and coordination with all other members. We have also held outreach dialogue of various forms and listened to the views and proposals of various parties.

尊敬的各位同事！在杭州峰会筹备过程中,中方始终秉持开放、透明、包容的办会理念,同各成员保持密切沟通和协调。我们还举办了各种形式的外围对话,倾听各方利益诉求。

I hope that during discussions in the coming two days, we will pool our wisdom and create synergy so as to enable the Hangzhou Summit to fulfil its mandate of boosting global growth, strengthening international economic cooperation and promoting the future growth of the G20.

我期待在接下来两天的讨论中,我们能够集众智、聚合力,努力让杭州峰会实现促进世界经济增长、加强国际经济合作、推动二十国集团发展的目标。

Let's make Hangzhou a new departure point, and steer the giant ship of the global economy on a new voyage from the shore of the Qiantang River to the vast ocean. Thank you.

让我们以杭州为新起点,引领世界经济的航船,从钱塘江畔再次扬帆启航,驶向更加广阔的大海！谢谢大家。

Now, let's proceed to our first session-policy coordination and break a new path for growth.

下面呢,我们开始第一阶段会议,讨论加强政策协调、创新增长方式。

来源:https://mp.weixin.qq.com/s/UfCmCIafMkrQsYOczrVikA

Appendix.2 Speech by Secretary of Provincial CPC Committee in the Mobilization Meeting for G20 Summit
G20 峰会筹备工作动员大会省委书记致辞

On December 1st, 2015, China officially took over the G20 presidency. On the morning of the same day, the Mobilization Meeting for the G20 Hangzhou Summit was held in People's Great Hall of Zhejiang Province. Mr. Xia Baolong, Secretary of provincial CPC committee and Director of the provincial standing committee attended the meeting and gave a speech. The speech is as follows:

2015 年 12 月 1 日中国正式接任二十国集团主席国。当天上午,G20 杭州峰会筹备工作动员大会在浙江省人民大会堂举行。省委书记、省人大常委会主任夏宝龙出席动员大会并讲话,以下为讲话全文。

Ladies and gentlemen,Dear Comrades,
女士们、先生们、同志们:

In G20 Antalya Summit, President Xi Jinping spoke highly of Hangzhou as "a paradise on earth with sceneries as beautiful as paintings" and he stressed "Hangzhou is a famous historical and cultural city as well as the city of creativity. It is firmly believed that the 2016 Summit will give you a unique charm combining history and reality." This poetic statement is filled with Mr. Xi Jinping's affection towards every hill, every river, every tree and every blade of grass in Hangzhou. Those words not only express the heartfelt praise and ceremonious recommendation, but also show sincere expectation for the success of the Summit and guide the direction of our work.

习近平总书记在安塔利亚峰会上,赞誉杭州"风景如画,堪称人间天堂",强调指出:"杭州是历史文化名城,也是创新活力之城,相信 2016 年峰会将会给大家呈现一种历史和现实交汇的独特韵味。"这诗一般的语言,凝结着总书记对杭州一山一水、一草一木的深厚感情,既是由衷赞美和隆重推介,也对办好 G20 峰会提出了殷切期望、指明了努力方向。

Hangzhou is like a classical book of history and humanity and its rich connotation makes us infatuated. From Kua Hu Bridege Civilization 8000 years ago to Liang Zhu Civilization 5000 years ago, from Wuyue Civilization

A Spot View of the Mobilization Meeting for the G20 Hangzhou Summit

G20 杭州峰会筹备工作动员大会现场

to Southern Song Dynasty Civilization, from the great emperor Qian Liu, who brought people welfare to the great patriot Yuefei, from the great Tang Dynasty's poet Bai Juyi to Song Dynasty's great litterateur Su Dongpo, from the great thinker Chang Tai-yen in Qing Dynasty to modern literature Lu Xun, from one of the most famous temples in south-east China, Lingyin temple to the holy land of China's Seal cutting culture, Xiling Society of Seal Arts, from the legendary Wan Song School to the well-known Zhejiang University, Hangzhou is a city with rich cultural heritages. Many masters and talented people made their life brilliant and influential in Hangzhou. We believe that Hangzhou will show its unique character as an ancient capital of China and a cultural resort during the Summit.

杭州恰如一部历史人文的经典藏书,她的底蕴让人迷恋。从 8000 年前的跨湖桥文化到 5000 年前的良渚文化,从吴越文化到南宋文化,从保境安民的钱镠到精忠报国的岳飞,从唐代诗人白居易到宋代文豪苏东坡,从明清思想家章太炎到近代文学家鲁迅,从东南名刹灵隐寺到金石圣地西泠印社,从充满传奇的万松书院到誉满全球的浙江大学,杭州有着弦歌不绝、薪火相传的文脉,杭州有着大师云集、人才辈出的辉煌,杭州有着独领风骚、弥足珍贵的遗产。我们相信,2016年峰会时的杭州,一定会呈现出千年古都、文化圣地的独特韵味。

Hangzhou looks like a scroll of nature landscape and its beauty makes people amazed. Hangzhou has West Lake which is always charming with either light or heavy make-up. The great tide of Qiantang River in Hangzhou is known as a wonder in the world. In Fuchun River, the mountain and the sky are melt into the landscape. The Qiandao Lake consists of thousands of islands with hazy landscape. The Tianmu Mountain is lush while the Beijing-Hangzhou Grand Canal is a busy channel. Also, in Hangzhou, we have Xixi Wetland with rippling rivulet blended with mist there. Those are the natural beauty of Hangzhou with rivers reflecting mountains and birds' twitter in fragrance of flowers; those are the exquisite beauty of Hangzhou with its generosity and elegance; and also those are the classical beauty of Hangzhou with water flowing beneath the small bridge and the winding path leading to a secluded place. We believe that Hangzhou will show its unique character as a city built upon mountains by rivers during the G20 Hangzhou Summit.

杭州恰如一幅钟灵毓秀的山水画卷,她的美丽让人惊叹。杭州有"浓妆淡抹总相宜"的西湖,有被誉为天下奇观的钱江潮,有风烟俱净、天山共色的富春江,有烟波浩渺、星罗棋布的千岛湖,有峰峦叠嶂、层林尽染的天目山,有千里通波、百舸争流的京杭大运河,还有一曲溪流一曲烟的西溪湿地,这就是杭州湖光山色、鸟语花香的自然之美,这就是杭州落落大方、楚楚动人的精致之美,这就是杭州小桥流水、曲径通幽的典雅之美。我们相信,2016 年峰会时的杭州,一定会呈现出山水相依、湖城合璧的独特韵味。

Hangzhou is like a beautiful and splendid paradise with much compliment on her prosperity. "Hangzhou has been a prosperous city since ancient times." The great poet of Song dynasty, Liu Yong, described Hangzhou like this, "The bridges painted with willows and frog, the wind curtain with green screens, the market displaying jewelries and the houses filled with silk and satin." Italian traveler, Marco Polo praised Hangzhou as "the world's most beautiful noble city of paradise" in Yuan Dynasty. Either numerous silk shops in Qing He Lane or tea plantations in the mountains alongside West Lake, either the popular Louwailou restaurant located in the mountain root or brilliant porcelains made by Northern Song Dynasty's official porcelain kilns, all of which witness the former prosperity of Hangzhou. Lofty bridges, weaving roads, skyscrapers tower into the clouds and crowed business centers are the representatives of Hangzhou's modern prosperity. We believe that Hangzhou will show the world her boom and prosperity during the G20 Hangzhou Summit.

杭州恰如一座美丽华贵的人间天堂,她的繁华让人赞美。"钱塘自古繁华。"

宋朝大词人柳永曾用"烟柳画桥，风帘翠幕，市列珠玑，户盈罗绮"来描绘杭州，元代意大利旅行家马可·波罗也曾用"世界上最美丽华贵的天城"来赞美杭州。清河坊鳞次栉比的绸庄，西湖边漫山遍野的茶园，孤山下高朋满座的楼外楼，南宋官窑里美轮美奂的瓷器，都见证了杭州昔日的繁荣。巍然屹立的一座座大桥，纵横交织的一条条路网，高耸入云的一幢幢大楼，熙熙攘攘的一个个商业中心，都在续写杭州今天的昌盛。我们相信，2016 年峰会时的杭州，一定会呈现出流光溢彩、日新月异的独特韵味。

Hangzhou is like a hymn for the booming times. Her creation and energy make people speak highly of it. People say that Hangzhou is a paradise for entrepreneurial innovation since the entrepreneurial and innovative spirit of braveness and pioneering is inherited from ancestors. Hangzhou nurtures companies with global reputation like Alibaba; Hangzhou creates some distinctive town for the development of various industries; Hangzhou is the habitat for entrepreneurs with dreams at home and abroad; and finally Hangzhou is the test field for many reforms. We believe that Hangzhou will show the world her all-embracing and pioneering features during the G20 Hangzhou Summit.

杭州恰如一首潮起潮涌的时代赞歌，她的创新活力让人推崇。人们都说，杭州是创业创新的天堂。这里传承了敢为人先、勇立潮头的创业创新精神，这里孕育了阿里巴巴等享誉世界的知名公司，这里打造了引领产业发展的特色小镇，这里集聚了国内外心怀梦想的创客，这里落地了众多的改革试点，这里串起了驱动发展的创新走廊。我们相信，2016 年峰会时的杭州，一定会呈现出海纳百川、引领潮流的独特韵味。

Hangzhou is like the beautiful scenery in spring. People yearn for the happiness and harmonious life of Hangzhou. Hangzhou is the cradle of many good people and good deeds. We have "The Most Beautiful Mother" who sacrificed two hands to catch an unknown kid falling from 10th floor, "The Most Beautiful Driver" who stopped the coach to save the lives of his passengers at the end of his life and "The Most Beautiful Father" who jumped into chilling dam to save a strange little girl regardless of his own danger. Besides, there are many other great but ordinary people whose deeds moved us as well. Do boldly what is righteous, find happiness in helping others, be honest and trustworthy, and show care and love to elders and kids. The power of morality makes citizens of Hangzhou more kind and modesty to build the happiest and securest city in China so that everyone born in Hangzhou, studying in Hangzhou, working in Hangzhou and living in Hangzhou will be proud of it. We believe that Hangzhou will show the world her kindness, harmony and boundless love during the G20 Hangzhou Summit.

杭州恰如一道温暖如春的最美风景,她的幸福和谐让人向往。杭州是最美现象的发源地,是最美风景的主景区。我们有"最美妈妈"惊世一托,有"最美司机"忍痛一刹,有"最美爸爸"勇敢一跃,有"最美大学生"万里献血,我们还有更多的"最美普通人"见义勇为、助人为乐、诚实守信、尊老爱幼。无数杭州人身上汇聚着道德的力量,彰显着好人的风采,用质朴平实的言行,共同把杭州建设成了中国最具幸福感、最具安全感的品质之城。每一个生于斯、学于斯、工作于斯、生活于斯的人,都为此感到自豪、感到骄傲。我们相信,2016 年峰会时的杭州,一定会呈现出和谐友善、大爱无疆的独特韵味。

Dear comrades! To show the world the unique character of Hangzhou combining of history and reality is not only Mr. President's requirement, but also our target. 270 days later, the G20 Hangzhou Summit will open. We must earnestly implement president Xi's a series of important instructions and fully carry out the various policies by the central government about the G20 Hangzhou Summit. The whole province should work together to make good preparations for the Summit. Today, I want to emphasize five points for our preparation:

同志们! 2016 年峰会,杭州要向全世界呈现历史和现实交汇的独特韵味,这既是总书记对我们的明确要求,也是我们的不懈追求。现在离 2016 年峰会还有 270 天,我们一定要认真贯彻习近平总书记关于 G20 杭州峰会的一系列重要指示精神,全面落实中央的各项决策部署,举全省之力精心做好峰会筹备工作。这里,我强调五点意见:

Firstly, the G20 Hangzhou Summit is a political task assigned by the central government, so we must try our best to guarantee a successful summit. The preparatory work of the summit is an important mission of our work in this year and the next one. We should hold high standards, accelerate the speed, work down to earth, optimize the effect and spare no efforts to host a wonderful and successful summit with the significance as a milestone and the best impact. Only in this way can we meet the satisfaction of the central government, President Xi, foreign leaders, Chinese citizens as well as local people in our province.

第一，承办 G20 峰会是中央赋予浙江的一项重大政治任务，我们必须拿出百倍决心、付出百倍努力，把做好峰会筹备工作作为今年和明年一项重要工作，标准要高、速度要快、作风要实、效果要好，努力办成一届精彩、成功、具有里程碑意义、取得最佳成效的峰会，真正让党中央和总书记满意、外国元首满意、全国人民满意、全省人民满意。

Secondly, to undertake the G20 Summit is a great chance for the world to learn more about the charm of China and the features of Zhejiang Province. In that case, the G20 Hangzhou Summit should be a summit with high standards and local features. We should work hard to make it a first-rate summit to fully show the world the great achievement of the reform and opening-up policy, the great advantage of socialism with Chinese characteristics, the brilliant civilization of the state of courtesy, and the great achievement of Zhejiang Province featured "in practice and in the forefront."

第二，承办 G20 峰会是让全世界感知中国魅力和浙江风采的一个重要窗口，我们必须办出特色、办出水平，对照国际一流标准，查漏补缺、精准发力，努力使峰会充分展示中国改革开放的伟大成就，充分展示中国特色社会主义制度的巨大优越性，充分展示中华礼仪之邦的厚重底蕴，充分展示浙江"干在实处、走在前列"的优异成绩。

Thirdly, to undertake the G20 Summit is a test of our work in making a peaceful Zhejiang. We must keep eyes on the problems of security as playing chess carefully or fighting for a battle positively, make good preparation for controlling any potential danger and build up impregnable fortress of a secure summit and a stables society to ensure no risk at all.

第三，承办 G20 峰会是对平安浙江建设成果的一次集中检验，我们必须打起十二分的精神，绷紧安全稳定这根弦，下好先手棋、打好主动仗，把一切安全隐患消除在萌芽状态，牢牢筑起峰会安保和社会稳定的铜墙铁壁，确保万无一失。

Fourthly, to undertake the G20 Summit is a comprehensive inspection to the mental state of CPC members. That is a crucial battle field, so we must be brave to take the responsibility and attain the victory. We should display initiatives in helping out colleagues and fulfilling vacancies, work down to earth without chasing hollow reputation and cooperate together from leaders to grass-roots members, thus overcoming any difficulty with full energy to ensure a success summit with great working enthusiasm.

第四,承办 G20 峰会是全面检验党员干部精神状态的一场攻坚战,我们必须敢于担当、敢于胜利,主动补位、互相补台,埋头干事、不图虚名,上下同心、齐心协力,以最好的精神状态克服艰难险阻,以最大的工作热情推动峰会筹备工作顺利开展。

Fifthly, to undertake the G20 Summit is a great chance for Zhejiang Province to build a high-standard comprehensive well-off society. We must seize the opportunity and ride on the momentum to develop the chance and win the initiative of development for realizing the aim of build a high-standard comprehensive well-off society in the period of the thirteenth five-year plan. We should keep in mind that working down-to-earth and standing in forefront with new idea of development is our new creeds.

第五,承办 G20 峰会是推动浙江高水平全面建成小康社会的一次千载难逢的机遇,我们必须借梯登高、乘势而上,把握发展机遇、厚植发展优势、赢得发展主动,努力实现"十三五"时期高水平全面建成小康社会的奋斗目标,更好地扛起"干在实处永无止境,走在前列要谋新篇"的新使命。

Ladies and gentlemen, dear comrades! We firmly believe that after a nine-month struggle, a brand-new Hangzhou, a brand-new Zhejiang Province will appear in front of the world. We must react to people's trust and the given duty, and ensure the G20 Hangzhou Summit a distinctive success!

女士们、先生们、同志们! 我们坚信,经过 9 个月的拼搏奋斗,一个崭新的杭州、一个崭新的浙江将呈现在世人面前。我们一定会不辱使命、不负重托,让杭州 2016 年峰会呈现给世界一份别样的精彩!

英文来源:笔者翻译
中文来源:http://www.hangzhou.gov.cn/art/2015/12/2/art_812255_298000.html

Appendix.3 Selection of G20 Leaders' Communique Hangzhou Summit

《二十国集团领导人杭州峰会公报》

G20 Leaders' Communique Hangzhou Summit

4-5 September 2016

二十国集团领导人杭州峰会公报

2016 年 9 月 4 日—5 日

1. We, the Leaders of the G20, met in Hangzhou, China on 4—5 September 2016.

1.我们,二十国集团领导人,于 2016 年 9 月 4 日至 5 日在中国杭州相聚。

2. We met at a time when the global economic recovery is progressing, resilience is improved in some economies and new sources for growth are emerging. But growth is still weaker than desirable. Downside risks remain due to potential volatility in the financial markets, fluctuations of commodity prices, sluggish trade and investment, and slow productivity and employment growth in some countries. Challenges originating from geopolitical developments, increased refugee flows as well as terrorism and conflicts also complicate the global economic outlook.

2.我们相聚在全球经济继续复苏、部分经济体抗风险能力加强、增长新动能开始出现的时刻。但经济增长仍弱于预期。金融市场潜在动荡、大宗商品价格波动、贸易和投资低迷、一些国家生产力及就业增长缓慢等下行风险犹存。地缘政治走向、难民增加以及恐怖主义冲突等挑战导致全球经济前景复杂化。

3. We also met at a time of continued shifts and profound transformations in the configuration of the global economic landscape and dynamics for growth. With these transformations come challenges and uncertainties as well as opportunities. The choices we make together will determine the effectiveness of our response to the challenges of today and help to shape the world economy of the future.

3.我们相聚在世界经济版图持续变化和全球增长动力大转型的重要时刻。这一转变带来挑战和不确定性,同时也蕴含机遇。值此时刻,我们所做出的决定事关能否有效应对当今世界诸多挑战,也关乎如何塑造世界经济未来。

4. We believe that closer partnership and joint action by G20 members will boost confidence in, foster driving forces for and intensify cooperation on global economic growth, contributing to shared prosperity and better well-being of the world.

4.我们坚信,二十国集团建立更紧密伙伴关系,携手行动,将为世界经济增长传递信心,提供动力,增进合作,促进普遍繁荣,造福各国人民。

5. We are determined to foster an innovative, invigorated, interconnected and inclusive world economy to usher in a new era of global growth and sustainable development, taking into account the 2030 Agenda for Sustainable Development, the Addis Ababa Action Agenda and the Paris Agreement.

5.我们决心构建创新、活力、联动、包容的世界经济,并结合2030年可持续发展议程、亚的斯亚贝巴行动议程和《巴黎协定》,开创全球经济增长和可持续发展的新时代。

6. In this context, we, the G20, as the premier forum for international economic cooperation, forge a comprehensive and integrated narrative for strong, sustainable, balanced and inclusive growth, and thereby adopt the attached package of policies and actions—the Hangzhou Consensus—based on the following:

6.为此,二十国集团作为国际经济合作主要论坛,同意根据以下原则,就推动世界经济强劲、可持续、平衡和包容增长的一揽子政策和措施形成"杭州共识":

Vision. We will strengthen the G20 growth agenda to catalyze new drivers of growth, open up new horizons for development, lead the way in transforming our economies in a more innovative and sustainable manner and better reflect shared interests of both present and coming generations.

放眼长远。我们将完善二十国集团增长议程,发掘增长新动力,开辟新增长点,以创新和可持续的方式推动经济转型,更好地维护当代和子孙后代共同利益。

Integration. We will pursue innovative growth concepts and policies by forging synergy among fiscal, monetary and structural policies, enhancing coherence between economic, labor, employment and social policies as well as combining demand management with supply side reforms, short-term with mid- to long-term policies, economic growth with social development and environmental protection.

综合施策。我们将创新经济增长理念和政策,财政、货币和结构性改革政策相互配合,经济、劳动、就业和社会政策保持一致,需求管理和供给侧改革并重,短期政策与中长期政策结合,经济社会发展与环境保护共进。

Openness. We will work harder to build an open world economy, reject protectionism, promote global trade and investment, including through further strengthening the multilateral trading system, and ensure broad-based opportunities through and public support for expanded growth in a globalized economy.

扩大开放。我们将继续努力建设开放型世界经济,反对保护主义,促进全球贸易和投资,加强多边贸易体制,确保全球化背景下的经济增长提供惠及更多人的机遇、得到公众普遍支持。

Inclusiveness. We will work to ensure that our economic growth serves the needs of everyone and benefits all countries and all people including in particular women, youth and disadvantaged groups, generating more quality jobs, addressing inequalities and eradicating poverty so that no one is left behind.

包容发展。我们将确保经济增长的成果普惠共享,满足各国和全体人民尤其是妇女、青年和弱势群体的需要,创造更多高质量就业,消除贫困,解决经济发展中的不平等现象,不让任何国家、任何人掉队。

7. Our growth must be shored up by well-designed and coordinated policies. We are determined to use all policy tools—monetary, fiscal and structural—individually and collectively to achieve our goal of strong, sustainable, balanced and inclusive growth. Monetary policy will continue to support economic activity and ensure price stability, consistent with central banks' mandates, but monetary policy alone cannot lead to balanced growth. Underscoring the essential role of structural reforms, we emphasize that our fiscal strategies are equally important to supporting our common growth objectives. We are using fiscal policy flexibly and making tax policy and public expenditure more growth-friendly, including by prioritizing high-quality

investment, while enhancing resilience and ensuring debt as a share of GDP is on a sustainable path. Furthermore, we will continue to explore policy options, tailored to country circumstances, that the G20 countries may undertake as necessary to support growth and respond to potential risks including balance sheet vulnerability. We reiterate that excess volatility and disorderly movements in exchange rates can have adverse implications for economic and financial stability. Our relevant authorities will consult closely on exchange markets. We reaffirm our previous exchange rate commitments, including that we will refrain from competitive devaluations and we will not target our exchange rates for competitive purposes. We will carefully calibrate and clearly communicate our macroeconomic and structural policy actions to reduce policy uncertainty, minimize negative spillovers and promote transparency.

7.实现经济增长,必须加强政策设计和协调。我们决心将各自以及共同使用所有政策工具,包括货币、财政和结构性改革政策,以实现我们强劲、可持续、平衡和包容性增长的目标。货币政策将继续支持经济活动,保持价格稳定,与中央银行的职责保持一致,但仅靠货币政策不能实现平衡增长。在强调结构性改革发挥关键作用的同时,我们还强调财政战略对于促进实现共同增长目标同样重要。我们正在灵活实施财政政策,并实施更为增长友好型的税收政策和公共支出,包括优先支持高质量投资,同时增强经济韧性并确保债务占国内生产总值的比重保持在可持续水平。此外,我们将继续研究二十国集团在必要时可采取的适合各国国情的政策措施,以支持增长和应对潜在风险,包括应对资产负债表的脆弱性。我们重申,汇率的过度波动和无序调整会影响经济金融稳定。我们的有关部门将就外汇市场密切讨论沟通。我们重申此前的汇率承诺,包括将避免竞争性贬值和不以竞争性目的来盯住汇率。我们将仔细制定、清晰沟通我们在宏观经济和结构性改革方面的政策措施,以减少政策的不确定性,将负面溢出效应降至最低,并增加透明度。

8. We are making further progress towards the implementation of our growth strategies, but much more needs to be done. Swift and full implementation of the growth strategies remains key to supporting economic growth and the collective growth ambition set by the Brisbane Summit, and we are prioritizing our implementation efforts. In the light of this, we launch the

Hangzhou Action Plan and have updated our growth strategies, including new and adjusted macroeconomic and structural policy measures that can provide mutually-supportive benefits to growth. We will also strive to reduce excessive imbalances, promote greater inclusiveness and reduce inequality in our pursuit of economic growth.

8.我们在落实增长战略方面取得了新进展，但仍有大量工作需要推进。迅速和全面落实增长战略对于支持经济增长和实现布里斯班峰会制定的共同增长雄心仍然十分关键，我们正在明确落实增长战略措施的优先顺序。为此，我们制订了《杭州行动计划》并更新增长战略，包括新的和调整的宏观经济及结构性政策措施，发挥二者相互支持以共同促进增长的作用。我们还将致力于减少过度失衡，并在追求经济增长的过程中提升包容性和减少不平等。

英文来源：http://www.fmprc.gov.cn/mfa_eng/zxxx_662805/t1395000.shtml
中文来源：http://www.fmprc.gov.cn/web/zyxw/t1394916.shtml

References | 参考文献

[1]　《汉语世界》Hangzhou at a Glance［M］. 北京：商务印书馆,2016.

[2]　杭州市人民政府新闻办公室. 杭州［M］. 杭州：杭州出版社,2016.

[3]　杭州市人民政府新闻办公室. 印象杭州［M］. 杭州：杭州出版社,2016.

[4]　中国人民大学重阳金融研究院. 2016:G20 与中国［M］. 北京：中信出版社,2016.

[5]　陈婵,李雪,石杨,薛韪禾. 为西湖博览会打造英文名片——西博会相关人员实用英语手册［M］. 杭州：浙江工商大学出版社,2015.

[6]　李莹莹. 西湖传说文化探微［M］. 杭州：浙江工商大学出版社,2015.

[7]　董琇. 国际会议英语：程式与技巧［M］. 上海：同济大学出版社,2015.

[8]　胡庚申. 国际会议交流［M］. 北京：外语教学与研究出版社,2013.